W9-BBU-044

THE NO-SELF HELP BOOK

40 Reasons to Get Over Your Self & Find Peace of Mind

KATE GUSTIN, PhD

NON-DUALITY PRESS
An Imprint of New Harbinger Publications

Distributed in Canada by Raincoast Books

Copyright © 2018 by Kate Gustin
                  Non-Duality Press
                  An imprint of New Harbinger Publications, Inc.
                  5674 Shattuck Avenue
                  Oakland, CA 94609
                  www.newharbinger.com

Cover design by Amy Shoup; Acquired by Elizabeth Hollis Hansen; Edited by Jean Blomquist

Library of Congress Cataloging-in-Publication Data on file

20   19   18

10   9   8   7   6   5   4   3   2   1   First Printing

To the Great Mystery,
with gratitude
from a "spiritual being having a *human* experience."
(Pierre Teilhard de Chardin)

A human being is part of the whole, called by us "Universe," a part limited in time and space. He experiences himself, his thoughts and feelings as something separate from the rest—a kind of optical delusion of his consciousness. The striving to free oneself from this delusion...to try to overcome it is the way to reach the attainable measure of peace of mind.

—Albert Einstein

Contents

Part 1: Selfhoods

Part 2: No-Self Speaks

Part 3: To Self or Not to Self?

Foreword

Let's start off with a question to help you slap yourself across your face, in the most spiritual way imaginable, of course. Who would you rather live your life as?

1. Who you think you are?

2. Who you want to be?

3. Who you actually are?

Tuck your answer under your mala beads for just a second; we'll look it in the eyes in just a moment.

Hell isn't a fun place (just in case you thought otherwise). There's a lot of opinions about what hell is, ranging from being in an eternally overheated sauna, to being surrounded by noise when you just want to meditate or meditating when you're just craving noise, to being depressed or feeling empty inside. Yet, I dare say, what's more hellacious than all those terrible places that we visit from time to time is that trump card of hell we deal ourselves from the deck of life: "trying to be someone you're not."

Nobody knows the purpose of life…until this paragraph. (Just pretend I know this; it'll make this paragraph seem more impactful.) Maybe the purpose of life is for *you* to live *your* life. In other words, for you to deal yourself the heaven-on-earth card of graceful permission for *you to be you*. Similarly, maybe the purpose of a tree's life is for it to be the unique tree that it is. Not for it to think that it's a different kind of tree. Not for it to try to be a dolphin. And not for it to think it should be a dolphin tree or any other variation of the self-created hell that it might bring upon itself by trying to be something it's not. The sooner the tree can cut through the psychological scar tissue of thinking that it is something it's not, the sooner it can step into the peaceful flow of living its life by allowing itself to be what it already is: a tree.

You are a tree. That's who you really are, a tree. Just kidding, you're probably not a tree. Yet it would've been really convenient if you were a tree, because I think the tree analogy would've ended with a lot of literary authority—by me telling you that you're a tree. But this book that you're holding was probably made from a tree. Now you probably feel fully integrated with the tree metaphor, so you can realize you are not the tree literally—yet metaphorically, you definitely are the tree.

What was your answer to the slap-in-the-face question? Many of us are convinced that we are *who we think we are*. Like there's some kind of magical correlation between our sense of certainty around who we think we are and the truth of who we are. How much thinking, interpretation, stories, and reinforcement do you put into trying to be who you think you are? AND (written in all-caps so you know it's the beginning of a challenging proposition) what if who you think you are, your sense of self, isn't even close to who you really are? What if the sequoia believed with 100-percent certainty that it was an apple tree?

Or what about the option of putting your life force into living as *who you want to be*? This option is a glorious one, especially for us self-helpers who have taken steps of personal empowerment and probably have at least three vision boards in our trophy case. The excitement around deciding who you want to be and going after it with all of your intentionality, affirmations, and beliefs is sexy as hell. Yet no matter how sexy, it's still hell because it isn't you. The sequoia who wants to be a millionaire circus clown is still torturing itself with the betrayal of not allowing itself to discover and be who it really is.

What about the least ego-gratifying option, living as *who you actually are?* Maybe it's the most obvious choice to direct our mind and body resources in order to have a beautiful life, and that's what makes it the hardest to find. You were hiding in plain sight all along, but your awareness was blind to your obviousness because it was looking outward, into the thought fields and imagination, to your seductive mind's story of who it thinks you are or who it thinks you should be. Slicing through the stories and ideas about who you are, as well as your allegiance to them, means you transcend the hell of indifference of just settling for who you think you are. And you transcend the purgatory of arrogance that accompanies thinking you should be who you want to be or who others think you should be. It means you arrive at a place of humbleness in which you don't try to define who you are; you curiously discover who you are. And it's a place of courage where you don't just try to mentally comprehend who you are; you live who you are.

I can't be certain of anything because I am certain that I'm not certain of anything, yet I can say that in my experience, we are all our own unique version of the sequoia. When we realize that we have been beyond our own imagination of ourselves all along, we can let go of confining ourselves to the claustrophobic container that keeps us playing life small and take bold steps into the mystery of who we really are. While you will definitely encounter fears, insecurities, and challenges as you become the willing adventurer exploring the mystery of you, you'll very likely find the geyser of meaning and fulfillment that makes your life a much more enriched experience.

And into the journey of the mystery you go, wonderfully guided by Kate Gustin. My crystal ball tells me that you'll find a lot of fruit as Kate challenges you to level up your awareness to see the many nuances of the psychological hiding places you may be constructing to conceal yourself in while thinking you're the hiding place. As your awareness brings new daylight to an old reality, hell transitions to heaven as Kate then guides you to lean deeper into the mystery of you. Please make space for grief, anger, fear, insecurity, and relief as you dive in. True transformation is a courageous effort, not an easy one. Yet it's always meaningful. Sometimes we all need to slap ourselves in the egoic face to find our heart and soul. *The No-Self Help Book* is engineered to offer a phenomenal slap. Enjoy!

—JP Sears
Life coach and author of
How to Be Ultra Spiritual:
12½ Steps to Spiritual Superiority

Introduction

No-self?? What does that even mean? Aren't we simply born as a self?

Good question. Yes, we each assume that we are a self—an individual body complete with its very own individual mind, a two-in-one package. Being a self appears to be a given, a universal truth in the same camp as the sky is blue and gravity keeps us on the ground.

Have you ever wondered, though, what you would find were you to unwrap this all-too-obvious package of self? What would lie at the center, beneath the ribbons and bows, the cardboard box?

If you're like most people, you might argue that something solid and real exists inside. Not only that, you might say that this interior self constitutes the most important aspect of who you are. And an entire industry agrees with you. "Self-help" has been built around understanding this self and catering to its needs. Visit any bookstore and you will find a prominent self-help section dedicated to the self's cultivation and healing: texts on guiding the self out of hardship; transforming the self in and out of relationship; coaching the self to be more resilient, less angry, more assertive, less dependent, more loving, less addicted, more successful, less introverted, more productive, less distracted, more balanced, less reactive, more creative, less anxious, more happy…well, you get the idea.

Should we gather from the hundreds of troubleshooting manuals in print that the mysterious contents of our self-box are defective?

Personally, I do not believe so. And professionally, after working for years as a psychologist at a medical center's department of psychiatry, I have not found any evidence to suggest that people are fundamentally broken or damaged at the core. In fact, I have not found any evidence proving that a tangible self exists at the core at all.

No self? But what's the alternative?

I hear you. And I, too, can appreciate the apparent absurdity of it. But this is where it gets interesting. We are learning from psychology and neuroscience, and from carefully looking at our own experience through fresh eyes, that we are not who we think we are.

Humanity has been brainwashed by the inner voice of the mind, the one that accompanies us 24/7 and comments on our every waking moment. The one that narrates our thoughts and feelings and then offers a critique about them, telling us what we *should* be thinking or feeling. The one who labels us as "not enough" or "better than" and dishes out silent judgment toward others.

This inner voice—which we believe to be that of our *self*—has trained us to relate to it as if it were a solid nugget residing somewhere in our brain. And yet, that voice in the head is a *story* of who we are, not *really* who we are.

The self is like the announcer of a ball game—announcing each play as it occurs, providing background information about the athletes, speculating about the season's prospects, creating the overall story of the game. But the story of the game is obviously not the game itself. The game happens independently of whether the announcer is present or not. The self-commentator has mistaken itself as the ball game, which is to say that, collectively, we have mistaken the voice in our heads as our true being.

Such mistaken identity comes at a cost. The self-voice, though quite capable of being affirming, inspiring, and constructive, often generates a distressing torrent of worry and second-guessing, shaming and blaming, regret and guilt. No one's self is immune to the unrelenting barrage. Here's a sampling of my self's outpouring: *Should I be outing myself publicly as not having a self? What will book reviewers think? What will my parents think?*

While such *shoulda, woulda, coulda* mind-chatter may seem innocuous, self-talk, over time, tends to turn into unhealthy narratives. It becomes the source of emotional pain and impairment. For instance, a retired paramedic entered my office with a self-story that he must rescue others in order to be of value. Physically incapable of performing anymore as a first responder, he struggled with depression, unable to update his heroic self-narrative to acknowledge his maturing stage of life and his other valuable roles and contributions. This left him feeling stuck and helpless, paralyzed by his mind's judgment of himself as useless.

Here's another example of the potency of the mind's narrative. A middle-aged woman who was sexually assaulted decades ago met with me to address eating and weight issues. She unconsciously continued to hold the belief that she needed to be obese in order to be unattractive and, thus, invisible to society and safe from future assault. Her weight complicated her diabetes and other significant health problems, but her self-story told her that losing pounds would only make her vulnerable to being victimized again by others. For this reason, she continued her unregulated, harmful eating habits.

We can see that the mind-made self can spin a complex and often problematic narrative out of the circumstances of our lives. Decades of psychotherapy and self-help practices have shown that we do have the ability to talk back to the mind and reconfigure this narrative more constructively. We can mend the story of the wounded self, the addicted self, the fearful self. But no matter how much reauthoring we do, the self will continue to spin out its sticky stories. And we will continue to buy into them.

Until we don't.

Until we disentangle ourselves from the self's web altogether.

How?

By not taking the self's stories at face value, as literal truth. By disidentifying with the voice in our heads rather than endlessly analyzing or doctoring it. By no longer assuming the mind to be who and what we are.

Well…maybe, but who am I then, if not the self in my head?

Another good question.

For thousands of years, the human race has grappled with the ultimate inquiry: *Who am I?* Prominent religious leaders, spiritual teachers, philosophers, scientists, and academics of all stripes have tried to describe the essential human ingredients that not only differentiate our species from others, but that also distinguish each individual person as unique. From the Buddha to Lao-tzu, from Hume to Hegel, from Jung to Einstein, the self has been the subject of considerable discourse.

Yet, despite centuries of theorizing, investigating, and debating, no clear consensus has emerged as to the essential nature of the self. Some regard the self as a tangible, material form: a bunch of muscles and bones and organs encapsulated by skin, known as the physical body-mind. Others see it as a dynamic, unfolding process, not a concrete thing but an ongoing life narrative. Still others, especially those within Eastern wisdom traditions, view the self as complete illusion, an empty eye of a hurricane of circulating thoughts, emotions, and sensations.

Western tradition privileges a view of self as linked to an autonomous ego and rational thought, à la Aristotle and Descartes. Yet those now investigating the "anthropology" of the self have begun to view the self more as a system constituted by its environment. Advances in neuroscience have contributed to this understanding of the experiential and contextual self.

Such a wide range of opinion about the self is not surprising when we remember that a psychologist will view it through a different lens than will a minister than will a professor of philosophy. But, regardless of who's looking at the elusive self, there's no question that it can be a troublemaker. The self, as it's conventionally experienced on a day-by-day basis, can be nosey and opinionated, oversensitive and prickly. It frequently butts into business where it doesn't belong, personalizing events and feeling persecuted. This book explains why and how we may be better served without the self.

That being said, *The No-Self Help Book* is not intended as pop puritanical doctrine, endorsing a denial of basic emotional, physical, and social needs. In fact, I've met with too many clients who've suffered from self-effacement and an underdeveloped sense of their personal rights. They tend to negate their own priorities and unknowingly defer to others, often at their own expense. In extreme cases, such self-abdication can make these individuals more vulnerable to being used or abused by others.

So, to be clear, *The No-Self Help Book* is not about neglect of the individual. A certain baseline of personhood needs to be in place to take care of one's body, relationships, and daily functioning. Such primary ego development is a prerequisite for mind-body well-being and healthy individuality. *The No-Self Help Book* respects the endeavor of ego development, essential as it is for skillfully navigating the challenging quandaries, disappointments, and losses of our lives. But there are plenty of other resources for that.

This book delves a bit deeper, beyond the realm of basic ego functioning to see exactly what is the driving force underneath. It investigates the inclusive consciousness at the root of our mistaken notions of a separate, ego-based self. And, rather than being "above it all" or a spiritual bypass of daily concerns, The No-Self Help Book is about learning how we can participate in the compelling and often tumultuous events of our lives without taking the mind's commentary about these proceedings too seriously. In other words, we don't have to throw the baby (our personal subjectivity) out with the bathwater (unnecessary identification with self-stories).

Outline of Sections

Each brief chapter identifies a reason why the troublemaker self is optional, why we don't need it. Part 1, "Selfhoods," establishes the constructed nature of this phantom entity and lists the ways in which it can hinder us.

Part 2, "No-Self Speaks," introduces an antidote to the problematic self: no-self. The term "no-self" is Buddhist in origin, derived from the Pali word *anatta* and the Sanskrit word *anattman*, both meaning "not self." According to Buddhist doctrine, we correctly perceive the existence of our body, sensations, emotions, thoughts, habits, and awareness, but then we mistakenly conclude that they are our true nature.

Like the term "self," no-self has been described in many ways: emptiness, primordial consciousness, unity realization, nonlocalized field of awareness, oneness, or simply as the absence of a self-referential construct ("I") in mental activity. But here's all you need to know about no-self: as we disidentify with our false self, we can begin to live as what we actually are. Part 2 describes the many attractive features of what we actually are when the veil of self has been removed. All of the chapters in this section are written directly from no-self's voice (as indicated by a change in font).

The third and final section of *The No-Self Help Book*, "To Self or Not to Self?" helps you decide whether *selfing*—the process of buying into your self-story—has been useful for you. Has it increased your happiness and life satisfaction? Is it worth continuing to invest in the self you have built?

At the end of the book, you will find the "MeSearch" addendum that provides a selection of research findings related to each chapter's theme, offering a glimpse into the knowledge base about the self as it's been investigated in such fields as cognitive science, neuroscience, and psychology. Scientific studies lend an empirical perspective to the conversation. However, the studies chosen here represent a small sampling of the vast research available on each topic, and the findings are not cited with the intention of confirming the self's illusory nature or confirming no-self's existence, for that matter. Research can still help illuminate consciousness, if not charged with proving it. And the realms of science and spirituality can coexist within their own valid, if at times separate, domains upon the larger globe of truth.

A Much Greater Union

In a nutshell, the mission of *The No-Self Help Book* is essentially to enable people to have informed consent about their identity.

Long ago without knowing it, we entered into a marriage with the self. Never did we consciously agree to the union, let alone to a "'til-death-do-us-part" commitment to it! This book allows us to take stock of the default marriage that has wedded our sense of being to the mind's storytelling. It enables us to stand back and ask: "Has it been a collaborative partnership? Would we choose the same spouse today?"

If the answer is no, then the good news is that you don't have to. *The No-Self Help Book* allows for a conscious uncoupling from this bond to the self. While we can't turn off our thought process (nor would we really want to), we can end our disempowered relationship with it.

Without spousal obligation to the self, we can come to know ourselves as no-self, or as other-than-mind. We can then wed with a spaciousness of spirit, abiding, as it were, in a much greater union.

Part 1

Selfhoods

The truth is *we have all been taken over*! An identity theft has occurred within our very own heads. The culprit?

The self. The voice of our thoughts.

The clever mind has generated a thinking process so compelling and seemingly continuous that it has taken on a life and label of its own: "self." The seat of our thoughts has insidiously granted itself such convincing personhood that it seems outrageous to even question the self's validity in the first place.

But, if we look closely, we can see that, other than the conditioned thought forms out of which it is constructed, the self lacks substance. And yet, we have bestowed this etherlike entity—a collection of thoughts in our heads—the privilege of claiming to be who we are!

In buying into the mind's narrative, its language-based story about our experience, we have come to identify with a mere fraction of the limitless expanse of our spirit, intelligence, and potential.

The chapters in part 1 call the self on its shady business. We'll examine the many falsehoods propagated by the mind, the greatest of which is the existence of a separate self. Most of us automatically, unknowingly, subscribe to these falsehoods, which we'll call *selfhoods*. We unconsciously live within the narrow and often unhappy confines they afford us.

But please don't take my word for it. As you read through part 1, see if the self has duped you, too. Check out whether it has co-opted your most basic assumptions about who you truly are.

1.   The Imposter Self

Like the mythical Wizard of Oz, the self projects presence and power. But when we pull the curtain to the side and look closely within ourselves to locate the person behind the projection, we find…no thing!

Go ahead, look in the mirror. When you look directly into your eyes, at the awareness looking back at you, what *thing* do you see? No doubt, you will see a face and a body to which you can assign all sorts of attributes such as eye color, age, height, ethnicity, gender. But what about the consciousness, the awake intelligence itself that peers out knowingly through your eyes? Does that have color, age, height, ethnicity, gender?

According to modern neuroscience, the self is less a thing than it is a process. In the process of *selfing*, the mind links together separate moments of subjectivity to give us the impression that we are a coherent, enduring entity.

When we think about ourselves, we activate a self-representation in the brain, a feeling of "me." But just because we have a feeling of "me" in the mind does not mean that a real self exists separate from the realm of thought. For example, we can hold a compelling image of a superhero in our minds without it pertaining to anything real outside our imagination. Thinking about Superman does not make him exist. When we're not explicitly thinking about ourselves, our sense of self vanishes and our mind-body continues to function just as well without it. The self, like Superman, is a mental creation, a story.

Despite our ego's posturing, no solid self actually lies within us. Investigate for yourself: When you wake up in the morning, does the self (the narrative voice in your head) have to tell you to get up, or do you just open your eyes? When you feel sad, scared, or excited while watching a movie, are those feelings orchestrated by the self, or do they arise spontaneously? When you hug someone you care about, does the self command you to do it? Does the self manufacture each flash of insight you're graced with? Was it responsible for the raw sensory experience of your most recent meal, for the awe you felt when you last saw a beautiful sunrise?

And yet the self ends up taking credit for all of it. Every occurrence, every accomplishment, the self claims as its handiwork. It's no wonder that most people who come into my office tell me that they feel like a fraud, an imposter.

The "imposter syndrome" was identified forty years ago by psychologists investigating why many people often feel like they're pretending, and why they have trouble taking their successes seriously. Though psychologists originally believed the syndrome was caused by a deficit of achievement-related self-worth, the epidemic prevalence of self-doubt experienced by those with the syndrome seems to suggest a deeper root. When you consider that the self does commit fraud as it masquerades as something more than myth and metaphor, it's not surprising that insecurity due to feeling like an imposter would proliferate.

The fact is it's the *self* that is the imposter! The voice of our thoughts performs a dazzling act of wizardry by convincing us that *it* authors our lives. This is the shocking reality beyond the curtain: our subjectivity operates without a subject at the controls behind it. When it comes to the self, there's no *there* there!

2. The Self Slices and Dices

Selfing involves a never-ending process of differentiation: what-is-me vs. what-is-not-me. Division helps the self maintain the illusion of being a separate and real thing.

The self first divides the whole of creation's pie into "self" and "other." It does this so automatically and instantaneously that such division appears absolute, a basic truth of experience.

The self then sections out broad categories in the "other" half: living vs. inert, animal vs. vegetable vs. mineral, skyscape vs. land-scape, and so on. Each of these categories is fractionalized further into an explosion of infinitesimally specialized pieces: paring vs. butter knife, the neighbor's golden retriever vs. your poodle Bingo, 10,560 different species of fern. The self declares with 100 percent psychological and epistemological certainty, that it (the "I") is not any of these pieces.

Instead, the self turns to its own half of the pie. The "self" half also undergoes the mind's chopping blade: ideas vs. feelings vs. sensations, id vs. ego vs. superego, soul vs. spirit, to name a few arbitrary partitions. Emotions may be extracted into meticulous and measure-able slices (doubt vs. fear vs. regret vs. shame vs. anger vs. exaspera-tion), as may thoughts (expectations vs. plans, memories vs. ruminations) and aspects of personality (optimism, neuroticism, extroversion).

This delicious multiplicity and nuance of creation is not the issue. If the self were to celebrate it (or, better yet, identify as all of it), there would be no problem. But the self identifies, instead, with a mere fraction of what one truly is. The self gets lost in its dizzying self-other calculus and ends up feeling alienated and insignificant.

Here's an example. When going through a difficult time, we tend to focus on the painful emotions we're experiencing—for instance, our anger or depression or anxiety. The self equates itself with its mood (for example, "I *am* depressed," "I *am* angry"). This languaging, whether unconscious or conscious and articulated aloud, reflects how the mind reduces the "I" to a temporary feeling state. "I am unhappy" conveys that *I = unhappiness*.

It's not just semantics. Many people mistake their experience in the moment for the whole of their being. Clients with chronic pain struggle to remember the qualities of who they are above and beyond the pain they're in. People going through relationship breakups disproportionately factor despair or self-loathing into their self-concepts. Overidentification with physical and emotional states often comes at the expense of remembering one's enduring values; one's creativity, kindness, and contributions; one's dreams and aspirations.

You are much larger than a momentary expression of the mind-body. When you stop identifying with the self's slicing and dicing, you grant the seamlessness of life around you a chance to make your acquaintance. You come into contact with a sustaining wholeness that fills in the gaps of divisive states of mind.

3.   The Self Freezes

Each day we are exposed to tens of thousands of images and symbols that bombard the field of our awareness. We call these instantaneous bursts of mental activity *thoughts*.

The self is notorious for buying into the content of its thoughts: *I think it, therefore it's true*. A slight variation on Descartes, but essentially the same premise: that our thinking defines us and our world.

That the self holds great stock in the words passing through the mind is not surprising, since the self is entirely composed of language. What exactly are these thoughts from which the self derives a sense of identity? Imagine pausing or freezing your high-speed thinking process for a moment. Imagine opening up your mind like a freezer door and examining the contents. What would you find inside?

If you're like most freezers, subject to accumulation and neglect, your shelves might be crowded with the cold, crusted past, the boxed butter of old grievances: *How dare Carla not invite me to her New Year's party in eleventh grade! How unfair to not have made the badminton team, the drama club, the a capella group!*

You might encounter Tupperwared regrets, leftover entrées unsuitable for consumption: *I should have taken two years off from school and joined the Peace Corps back in my twenties. If only I had said I was sorry about what happened, we might still be friends.*

Don't forget the expired bag of peas in the corner that once may have iced wounds but never actually nourished you: *If I had just had a different or better parent, teacher, boss, body, luck…this probably wouldn't have happened to me.*

Keep looking through the freezer of your thoughts and you might also find it stocked with worry Popsicled on the door's shelves: *What if this fever doesn't go down? What if I get a negative performance review tomorrow?* Conjecture might be cubed in the ice trays, ready to cool down your next vital moment: *He probably won't find me attractive. Maybe I shouldn't sign up; I never win anything anyway.*

And then there are the judgments—those unhealthy staples—that command much of the freezer's space: *My body is getting wrinkled and flabby, and so is yours! Bob should just get over the breakup and move on already. Why is this person on the road in possession of a driver's license?*

Nor can we ignore the random song lyric or commercial ditty or rogue dirty word or naughty fantasy that creeps in and crystalizes in the cracks along the edges.

Yes, there are many cherished life memories in the freezer as well: *my first friend, pet, recital, ball game, kiss; watching baby pigs being born at midnight on auntie's farm; graduations, birthdays, weddings.* These we'd never want to be without.

On the whole, most mental content expires quickly and can be released back into the ether from whence it came. However, the self privileges every thought as essential fact and warehouses it in memory's freezer. And it remains loyal to its frozen peeps. The self continues to identify with the sweet-and-sour meatballs from five years ago when the relationship ended. It continues to contemplate the tasteless lasagna from last March when you were unfairly laid off from work.

Think about the thoughts your self has stored in the freezer. If you had to conduct an inventory of this frozen wasteland, how many of these thoughts would actually qualify as important or urgent? How many of these petrified expressions of the fluid mind would survive a thorough thawing and still be deemed useful?

4.   The Dictator Self

The self tends to direct our mental and emotional processes like a dictator. The selfing function (the "I" or "me" commentator) often takes unilateral control of decision making and bosses the mind-body around.

How?

Just consider a decision you have to make—something simple like whether to eat dessert tonight. As the self debates whether to end dinner with the apple tart, it prioritizes particular emotions and reflections in its thought process. On the one hand, the self may be swayed by fears associated with increased caloric intake and body image, for instance. On the other hand, the self may be motivated to maximize its serving size, given that it got a smaller slice of cake yesterday than other people did. Whatever the content of the self-talk, the point here is that the inner commentator assumes authority over the final dessert decision.

But how else would a decision get made?

If the self operated more as a parliamentary process than a dictatorship, for instance, decisions might be informed by greater representation from other mind-body constituents such as physiology ("Am I still hungry?"), curiosity ("What does it taste like?"), or intuition ("Perhaps it's not so much dessert I'm needing right now—is there something else I really need?"). The same thought associations about the apple tart would still be activated, but the self wouldn't get to prioritize these without input from other mind-body constituents. Shame-ridden stories about being perceived as a glutton or guilt-ridden narratives about one's thighs would not weigh in to the decision like special interests to the dictator. They would be factored alongside all other considerations, preventing marginalization of any part of the organism—heart, body, mind, or soul.

When the dictatorial self calls the shots, it drowns out other subtler voices of internal wisdom and guidance. A self with an over-bearing work ethic, for example, may override the body's signals of exhaustion and demand that one go to work even when sick. Or, a self determined to no longer be single may turn a blind eye to the early red-flag warnings of being in relationship with that handsome felon.

The self would do well to share its authority, as a more represen-tative form of government within the psyche would allow for sounder decision making. Try this out: when you're about to take action, take a moment to check in with all your constituents. Let your core values submit a vote about what job to choose, for instance, alongside that of the self. Your values might emphasize work that's service related, let's say, whereas the self might emphasize the job's salary or prestige. Your heart's longings and intellectual aspirations also get to cast their votes, chiming in about a livelihood that inspires and stimulates. All body-mind components representing the practical, spiritual, creative, and artistic sides of you get to come to the parliamentary table and offer their input.

Like many an autocrat, the self, when left to its own devices, will not just step down. It prefers to have its conditioned beliefs dictate the choice of one's livelihood, partner, lifestyle. Uncontested, the self will maintain its self-anointed rank and privilege as sovereign ruler of consciousness.

5. The Self Seeks Esteem

Envision, if you will, a black hole. Imagine this black hole inside you. It could be located in the middle of your brain, or perhaps deep within the gut, or in the heart area of your chest. Wherever it resides, it exerts a force that draws your past good deeds into its center.

All your successes, your strengths, and your positive qualities get pulled in: your school lap-a-thon certificate, your volunteering hours, your guitar recital, your patience with your little sister, your advanced credentials, the promotion you got at work, your recycling. But no matter how large the assortment of accolades, the black maw attracts more. The force of its voracious intake increases exponentially with the amount of personal accomplishment it consumes.

This imploding star is self-esteem, or, more precisely, the seeking of self-esteem. At the center lies a phantom metaphor, a bottomless singularity that threatens to eat you out of house and home. In other words, self-esteem is elusive; it's the promise of a certain feeling toward oneself that can never be reached. And the striving to reach it becomes quite costly, with the self directing vast quantities of time and energy into pursuing it.

In this way, the seeking of self-esteem represents a never-ending self-help project extraordinaire. I've met with hundreds of clients over the years who've struggled with a perceived lack of self-esteem, insisting that they could not pursue their career, relationship, or health goals until they acquired enough of it. Many become stuck in a holding pattern, waiting for the buildup of a critical (yet vague) mass of confidence before taking action.

But confidence, like self-esteem, is a way of relating to oneself, not a concrete achievement that one can hold in hand. The seeking of self-esteem can, thus, be more accurately understood as a *process*, just as selfing is a process. Self-esteem itself cannot be found anyplace within the psyche. There is no "esteem" enclave inside us that necessarily bloats or gloats after achieving enough weight loss or scoring enough investments.

Understanding this liberates us from the pursuit of self-esteem as an object to be acquired. Rather than striving to achieve full and final satisfaction with your productivity, your character, your conduct—because, really, when does that happen?—you can focus instead on the spirit in which you go about attending to your productivity, character, and conduct. Shifting the emphasis from the final self-esteem goal to the cultivation of skillful living, defining one's values and acting in line with them, is what actually enables the development of confidence.

6. The Self Wants

I recall watching my neighbor's two-and-a-half-year-old son standing next door on the driveway crying "I want" over and over again. It was a late summer afternoon, and he and his father had just played a game of catch. With ball in hand, he wailed "I want!" repeatedly, without saying what it was that he wanted or how much of it or when he'd like it. There was no object specified at all, only a pleading *wanting* coming forth unhappily from his mouth until finally silenced with a gentle hug by his father.

Selves want. They want things like cars and money and furniture. They want recognition and entertainment. They want comfort and pleasure. They want others to change. They want to be loved. The target of the wanting may vary, but the wanting does not. It hums in the background like a grating lawnmower on a Saturday morning, disrupting everyone's peace of mind.

Perpetual wanting is natural, even inevitable, given the self's essentially empty core. To compensate, the self attempts to accumulate what it can: material items, pleasurable mood states, reassurance, and security. Unfortunately, each desire met is quickly followed by another desire unmet. Have you noticed this? It usually takes just hours, if not minutes, before the sense of wanting resurfaces and attaches to the next desired thing.

Often when clients enter therapy, they assume that the treatment will help them get what they want, including finding the happiness they've been missing. Like most of us, they believe that happiness stems from having what one wants. But wanting is a moving target. A more reliable approach to well-being focuses on identifying and living the values that underlie the specific desires. For example, a person may want to take a trip to the coast or the mountains. This desire represents a larger value they hold—let's say, for adventure or love of nature. Even if one is not successful at acquiring the object of their desire (that is, being able to go on the trip), the underlying value continues to hold meaning. Desires tend to change, whether or not they're gratified. But values, often in the service of long-term qualities of being (such as creativity, adventure, fitness, learning, service, and the like), continue and can be honored in a range of ways.

Focusing on enduring values enables us to enjoy the process of our lives rather than having our happiness contingent upon momentary outcomes, the meeting of a specific goal or want. Wants are inexhaustible. A truly therapeutic approach to happiness, therefore, involves disengaging from the self's mission to get enough of what it *wants* or, for that matter, from its eternal quest to *be* enough.

7. The Self *Needs*

The self tends to equate what it wants with what it needs. In doing so, it experiences a sense of imperativeness, even entitlement, in meeting these needs. The transition from wants to needs may be a subtle one, but the result—a self on a mission to honor and fulfill its *needs*—is far from subtle. Just visit a shopping mall on the day after Thanksgiving.

Certainly, needs do exist. As body-minds vulnerable to the demands of biology, we do need food, water, shelter. As primates who evolved in tribes, we do have social needs for attachment and connection. The human body-mind prioritizes such needs naturally, automatically seeking food if hungry, water if thirsty, shelter if cold: bodies take care of themselves.

But the self is not the body. It is an overlay, a narrative that has convinced us that it requires the same attention and care as if it were a human being in its own right.

The illusion of the self's existence demands continual maintenance, with a long list of "necessities" to attend to: *I need to be liked. I need to be challenged. I need to be successful.* Just as with wants, the list of needs goes on and on. The vast majority of these items do not constitute survival needs. Yet the self feels as if they do and will elevate its language to make the case for securing them. The morning latte becomes a "requirement." Telling off one's grating coworker becomes an "honesty mandate." Shaming one's spouse into being more considerate about the clothes on the floor is simply speaking one's "truth." Suddenly, relative wants have been reframed as absolutes that the self must dutifully comply with.

Can you recall ever conflating your wants with needs? What about that weekend away? Was that truly a survival requirement? Or the larger, higher-resolution television? Or the acknowledgment you desperately wanted from your employer, your spouse, your mother-in-law?

To be clear, it's valid and healthy to have preferences and to pursue them, to actively shape the course of one's life. But, when the self brands preferences as *needs*, it can lead to a great deal of striving and accumulation, and, in the end, a sense of deprivation. Conflict and competition arise as well when others fail to register or comply with the self's *needs*.

At the root of its needing, the self is just trying to flesh out something that has no inherent meat to it. For this reason, even after having prioritized its wants, *needs*, TRUTHS, or COSMIC CALLINGS, the self lands, at the end of the day, like a hamster on a wheel, no closer to contentment.

8. The Self Whines

When are we going to get there?

Who wants to know?

The self, of course, wants to know. And, if it's coming from my eight-year-old son's self, it will repeat the question at three-minute intervals all the way to the campground, unless we implement an arsenal of distracting snacks.

The self likes to know things. It wants to know *when*, *where*, and most especially *why*. The innate curiosity of the human mind is a beautiful drive, the force behind limitless inquiry and invention.

But what happens when the self doesn't get an answer, or at least not the answer it wants?

But why did the ice cream cone fall? Because you were holding it to the side.

But why didn't yours fall? Because I was holding mine upright.

But why is my ice cream on the floor? Because it fell.

But why? It happens.

But yours didn't fall. No, it didn't.

Why not? I guess I was paying attention.

It's not fair. You're right.

The plaintive *why* can, thus, serve as a form of protest: a whining refusal to meet life on its own terms. When reality shows up in a way that conflicts with the self's preferences, the self tries to squeeze out a rationale that will magically change circumstances more toward its liking. The self does not suffer helplessness gracefully. It will stubbornly fold its arms, puff out its chest, and resist what is. Rather than accept the chocolate-chip puddle on the floor and proceed back into the line for another scoop, the self will stand its ground and argue about the inherent unfairness of gravity.

Many clients approach therapy desiring to know *why* they are experiencing what they're experiencing. Why have certain conflicts arisen, why have certain symptoms emerged, why have certain patterns played themselves out over years? Often, an earnest and important desire to understand oneself better and prevent future struggles drives such inquiry. And identifying the root of a problem is useful, of course, in helping determine appropriate treatment.

And yet, the *why* question frequently fronts more as a grievance, an expression of blame, regret, or exasperation with life's unfolding. Answering the *whys*, to the extent they can be answered, comprises only part of the healing. *Whys* are oriented toward the past. At some point, one must begin pivoting away from the *why* toward the present, toward the *what* and the *how*: *What does that mean for me now? How do I best go forward?*

9. The Self Is Picky

The self makes its way through life sorting through what it likes and dislikes, what it approves of and disapproves of. For the self, pickiness is an approach that pumps it up, makes it arbitrator of what is worthwhile and what is not.

Being discriminating grants the self a sense of stature and control, especially in an affluent, consumer-based culture that caters to individual preferences. (If you're not sure what I'm referring to, just consider it the next time you contemplate ordering a Midnight Mint Mocha Frappuccino Blended Coffee vs. an Iced Cinnamon Almond-Milk Macchiato at the local coffee shop.)

Pickiness becomes problematic, however, when the self projects its selectivity toward other people. At heart, the self simply wants to be accepted. And yet it ironically places countless conditions upon its acceptance of others:

He must be taller than me and in good health.

She must be multilingual and cultured.

They have to share my liberal-centrist orientation, but also be financially conservative.

Well-read—fiction doesn't count (and don't even mention memoir).

A professional, within the medical field ideally or perhaps law; interested in biking and movies and wine. Museums are a must— prefer modern art, but flexible.

Shops organic; vegetarian but not vegan.

Open-minded, generous, easygoing, inclusive, gracious, nonjudgmental.

The self's exacting criteria can be counterproductive. Its picky rule-outs may prevent most people from entering its inner sphere. Picking and choosing attributes in others as if shopping for an appliance reflects the self's presumption that people can be ordered by design and expected to perform accordingly. And then, when others don't comply, the self experiences not only disappointment but also outrage, as if one's consumer rights have been violated: *How dare he continue to be disorganized, short-tempered, introverted, noncommittal when I've invested so much time and energy in this relationship?*

And even if the formidable prerequisites are intended as a protective vetting, they end up further isolating the self. Indeed, the Western self currently suffers an unprecedented epidemic of loneliness. More people today live by themselves and report having a third fewer friends than a generation ago. Twenty-five percent report having no close friends at all.

The irony again, is that the picky self does not want its own features picked over. It longs to be received whole, as one package of personality and physicality, quirks, flaws, and predilections, the sum of many imperfect parts. It just has trouble extending the same allowance toward other people.

10. The Self Smirks

Smirk: where passive and aggressive meet on the face's landscape. The self will don this silent expression of condescension, a dismissive flare of the nostrils or pseudo half-smile, when the proper occasion arises. When feeling threatened by another's success, for example, the self attempts to remedy its own sense of inferiority by poo-pooing others. Why bother digging into the weedy roots of one's own inadequacy when the self can simply devalue the neighbor's garden with a look of feigned amusement or indifference?

The self routinely engages in social comparison to get its bearings. And yet such comparison tends to have the opposite effect, disorienting and demoralizing the self as it attempts to evaluate its standing vis-à-vis that of its siblings, peers, coworkers, community, nation, generation—the list goes on. Trying to broadly measure oneself against others is like comparing the proverbial apple and orange. Each person's makeup is indescribably unique, as are the circumstances of his or her upbringing and socialization. And yet the self is convinced that some types of fruit are inherently better than others—and it aspires to be among the chosen.

Even if the self does fare well in its own arbitrary comparisons, such ranking exacerbates rather than remedies the ego's inferiority complex. Rarely have I heard clients express how "everything's better" now that they found a new partner when their ex hasn't, or now that their earnings exceed that of their parents. The relative success appears to simply raise the bar of the self's expectations, creating a new yardstick by which to feel inadequate. There's always the next credential, the next promotion, more books to read, wittier comments to make, more funds to raise, a larger Facebook following to cultivate.

Furthermore, feeling at the top of one's game comes at a cost when the self does so through positioning others at the bottom. When the self smirks, it alienates itself from others. Acting superior doesn't make friends. Belittling others doesn't help one's loneliness. The dismissive facial shrug is but a Band-Aid balm that does nothing for the real wound—the self's smarting insufficiency.

11. The Self Strikes Out

Ever notice that you lash out in a manner that's out of proportion to the situation at hand? Or that you strike out more forcefully toward those you hold dearest?

Each person comes equipped with a hardwired emotional repertoire—a range of feelings that provide important information about the care of the body-mind. Emotions may tell us, for example, when comfort is needed, or when protection should be sought. Anger constitutes an essential part of this evolutionary survival kit, a signaling from within that appropriate self-defense or self-advocacy may be called for. Anger can mobilize us to respond to potential mistreatment or harm and, ideally, to safely prevent it altogether.

The self, however, has been known to strike out toward others unnecessarily. Evolutionarily speaking, getting angry at the customer service representative on the line, after thirty minutes of failing to navigate the company's phone tree, does not serve a protective purpose. And the school bully who threatens violence after not getting his way on the playground is not trying to prevent harm but rather to instigate it.

What causes the self to not play well with others?

The nature of the self is such that it relates *to* other selves rather than relating *as* other selves. This is to say that the self views itself as essentially separate from others, which means that, to connect with them, a bridge must be created and crossed. This approach to relationship is *inter*personal, or "between persons." Selves, standing on their islands of separateness, need things from each other relationally to feel whole. Personalities end up jockeying with other personalities to get perceived needs met. And when they don't get them, they can get angry.

It's a setup from the start, as approaching others for love immediately creates a precarious dependence. If one needs a friend's or relative's liking, love, or approval and doesn't receive it, hurt, resentment, or indignation can follow. Just think of how you felt the last time your phone call went unreturned, your birthday was overlooked, or your contribution went unnoticed.

Those in the inner circle tend to be the ones the self charges not only with its well-being, but also with its very psychological existence. When our nearest and dearest don't comply with mirroring our self and reinforcing its illusions, the self gets mad, even a bit frantic. Its veneer of self-sufficiency becomes threatened, its dependency revealed.

The anger experienced here is a triggering of the same evolutionary, physiological survival instinct. Needing others to confirm the self's existence activates the fight-flight-freeze reflex. While there's usually no actual threat confronting the body-mind, the self *feels* as if its very survival is on the line, and, in a psychological sense, it is: *Do I matter if you don't think I matter? Do I even exist if you don't notice me?*

Relating to oneself *as* love (discussed further in part 2) provides an alternative, enabling one to enter into relationship already whole. Approaching others as love from the outset prevents psychological dependency, decreasing the risk of striking out.

12. The Self Steals Credit

One can't even cross the street, carry on a conversation, or tend to one's hygiene without the self taking credit for it. Fancying itself the agent of all action, the self refuses to accept that the body-mind could navigate effectively on its own across the seas of relationship, livelihood, and self-care without its self-conscious deliberation. The self would have us believe that, without its input, we would devolve into couch-potato-hood.

And yet, our direct experience shows that there is an intelligence that directs our actions with or without engagement of the self's narrative. In other words, the self does not need to announce "I am thirsty" in order for the body-mind to secure a drink. We do not require the self's permission or commentary regarding the restroom to make appropriate use of it. The self-referencing circuitry of the brain does not control the reins of the horse.

The self would never know this because, first, it rarely stops its narrative long enough to find out what takes place without it. Second, it does not want to acknowledge an agency other than its own. It would be disempowering to discover that a flow of movement, an intercourse with life, happens naturally without its consent.

The self would rather continue stealing credit. Just watch: the next time you use your creativity, for example—writing a poem, painting a picture, playing an instrument, taking a photo, building something—notice where the inspiration comes from (or, rather, where it *doesn't* come from). Then see how quickly the self chimes in, stealing credit for the creation as if its overlay of thoughts were actually responsible for the recital of the "Moonlight Sonata" or for the watercolor abstract.

Observe, too, how the self so often offers critical commentary about "its" result: *I should have picked up the tempo; I didn't put enough blue in the composition; I can't write a decent line to save my life.* The self makes it all about the "I," even though, during the actual creative act, the concept of "I" (the story of the self) may not have even come to mind.

But the self continues to interpret all behavior as an exercising of its will, of its *trying*. Rather than acknowledge that doing happens (as the great mystic Yoda says, "There is no try"), the self maintains the convoluted view that "I make myself do."

13. The Self Is Selfish

'Nuf said.

14.   The Self Gets Rejected

The self likes to be liked. It wants to be included. We are, after all, social creatures having evolved in tribes. Relationships, however, become tricky, risky undertakings when the self steers them through the minefield of its sensitivities. The fragile self has a tendency to register interpersonal slights as personal rejection. Being unfriended on Facebook or not receiving a timely text can inflame deep-seated insecurities and diminish the self's delicate sense of worth.

The self assumes a perpetual DEFCON 1 defensive stance, continually scanning for signs of rejection. This hypervigilance creates a cycle of distancing: fear of rebuff generates a guardedness that makes others less likely to approach and engage, leading to further perception of rejection, alienation, and fortressing of the self.

In a perfect world, repeated experiences with attentive, reliable, loving caregivers would install within us a template for interpersonal trust and security during infancy and early childhood. Or, if this were not possible, a stable and affirming relationship with a significant other or dear friend later in life would serve the same purpose and mitigate the self's defensive structure.

But, as we know, relationships can be as unpredictable as the selves constituting them. And rejection (or perceived rejection) tends to make a disproportionately large imprint on the psyche. A single instance can overshadow many significant experiences of connection and belonging. Being publicly humiliated, being denied membership in a group, or being broken up with can be recalled with great pain and pixellation, while hundreds of occurrences of inclusion recede into the fog of the forgotten. Given the workings of mood-dependent memory, a recent slight can activate recollection of every past instance of rejection, disqualifying years of positive social interactions.

If the self had its way, it would require a guarantee of acceptance. It would want to know from the outset of each interpersonal encounter that it would be well-received. To prevent unnecessary vulnerability, the self might even engineer a contract. Who wouldn't want that—a pledge at the beginning of a relationship, or prior to its deepening, to ensure unconditional love and prevent the possibility of future rejection? An agreement designed with layers of formal protection, made official by decree of a judge or witnesses, legally contracted by the US government, spiritually ordained by religious doctrine, and sanctified by God, for better, for worse, for richer, for poorer, in sickness and in health, 'til death do you part...

Without such a contract (or even with one, but knowing the possibility of its dissolution), the self tightens the heart. It exposes as little surface area as possible to the pain of potential rejection.

15.   The Self Checks Out

The self has limited bandwidth for life's interference with its agenda. When that stress threshold gets crossed, the self seeks relief, an icing of its thwarted, inflamed ego.

Relief, of course, comes in various forms. Psychological escape can numb out the reality the self does not want to face. But, as we know, escape can be not only palliative but also addictive. The desire to check out (by nullifying the voice of the stressed-out self) gets reinforced by the quick reprieve it provides. Add the neurochemical stimulation of the brain's reward systems (which activate with certain numbing behaviors), and, before you know it, there's a habit in the making.

"What's the big deal?" the self may protest, arguing that it's entitled to improve its state of mind however it wants. After all, it needs a break and seeking refuge in some substance—a sugary confection, a good cup o' joe, a quick-acting sedative—is quite common.

At issue, though, is not the pleasure seeking per se, but the self's desire to escape itself. We don't need to blame or shame the self from some moralistic high ground. What's more effective is to examine what predisposes the self toward checking out to begin with. In therapy, clients explore the uncomfortable feeling states—such as boredom, loneliness, self-doubt, grief, or loss—that trigger an impulse to run away from those feelings.

For one man who felt disempowered in a stagnating marriage, gambling offered stimulation and a sense of possibility, even though the fallout from the slot machines caused significant financial stress and further relational paralysis. For another middle-aged client, a bottle of wine per night filled the nest left bare by her recently graduated son. A third client found that nighttime bingeing offered distraction from her chronic pain and a reprieve from the many struggles she faced each day as a result of her physical disabilities.

There are no quick fixes. When confronted with the hard, hard work of facing painful realities, the self often chooses to turn another direction. Reality, though, is not going anywhere. Troubling situations must be approached and confronted to be resolved or at least shaped into a state of affairs you can coexist with. Avoidance by the checked-out self, on its path to anywhere but the present moment, only delays the lasting peace of mind it seeks.

16. The Self Stays Stuck

The self prefers to stay put. Even though it may get caught up in its own whirlwind of wants and reactivity, it feels threatened by changes to its fundamental character and outlook. This makes perfect sense when we remember that, in order for the self to perpetuate the illusion of its existence, it has to project a certain consistency and cohesion across time. Change endangers that.

But, as we all know, everything changes: interest rates, batting averages, hair and skirt lines, television programming, entire fields such as science and health care. Paradoxically, change is one of the few reliable things we can count on, as the cliché goes. And yet there, among the shifting tumbleweeds of time, stands the unflinching self: a leathery cowboy declaring the durability of his doctrine, the solidity of his convictions, the intransience of his being.

How bold. How valiant. How delusional.

What the self does not see in the mirror is that even it is made up of ever-changing material: the regular turnover of thoughts, emotions, and sensory experiences. They all come and go through awareness, each just as impermanent as the next flower that blossoms and fades along the dusty road.

Ever find yourself attempting to prolong an experience that has already expired—trying to tell the same joke again or venting about the same grievance over and over, trying to ignite the same anger and righteousness? Or, what about maintaining a certain belief in the face of opposing evidence, denying warming trends while your toes become submerged in polar runoff?

To prevent change, the self warehouses its mental activity. It collects certain thoughts and perceptions and hangs them on countless walls of memory like a Louvre on steroids. The more emotionally charged the thought or experience is, in either an extremely positive or painful way, the more likely it will be displayed in this museum of selfhood.

Advances in neuroscience have revealed that traumatic events in particular can imprint themselves onto the cellular structure of the brain. Fortunately, animals, including humans, possess the ability to discharge energy from the nervous system and release traces of trauma from the mind-body after they occur. The sticky self, however, interferes with this healing process. Rather than directly experiencing and then discharging painful thoughts and emotions, the self tends to suppress them, which, in effect, binds those painful thoughts and emotions to the self. As the self then treads the corridors of its charged-memory museum, re-viewing the distressing events behind the glass, neural grooves get created in the brain, sensitizing the nervous system toward these events. Post-traumatic stress symptoms can develop in the wake of the self's interference in natural emotional processing.

The galleries of one's personhood, thus, tend to be biased toward extremes of the past—a life portrait of difficult feelings, controversy, tension, injury, and conflict, as well as ecstatic moments of intense joy, awe, pride. The self becomes stuck in curating the psyche's retrospective rather than allowing for a turnover of fresh showings in keeping with present-day experience.

17. The Self Second-Guesses

The self supervises every move it makes, looking over its shoulder like an unblinking parrot ready to chirp out the same annoying rebukes: *Should you have done that? Dessert again? Say something smart. Say something smart.*

The self's second-guessing tends to drown out quieter sources of feedback from the mind-body. Many clients come to therapy with distressing somatic complaints: debilitating headaches or muscle pain, irritable bowel or nausea, fatigue or rashes. These symptoms are often indicators of underlying emotional or psychological care that has been neglected, in addition to being signs of possible physical ailments. But the self, rather than listening to these messengers of stress, will second-guess them in various ways: minimizing the symptoms (*What's a little neck pain?*); creating a Marine rationalization for them (*Pain is just a sign of weakness leaving the body*); or shaming oneself for even considering responding to them (*You need to just put your big-girl pants on and get over it*).

The self also tends to second-guess attempts to re-evaluate decisions it's made. Being consistent lends the self a crucial sense of continuity, so it tries to abide by its original choices even when circumstances change. For example, a number of clients have reported staying in unsatisfying, unhealthy relationships for years because they didn't want to face having made "the wrong choice." Here, the self views a change in partnership as representing an error in judgment, a lack of resolve or steadfastness—basically an indication of the self's failing.

Saving face and making a good impression also fuels much second-guessing. The self often reviews its past encounters like the harshest movie critic. In the mind's slow motion, the self scrutinizes each frame of its interaction, delivering a blow-by-blow account of wrongdoing: *I can't believe I said "It's been a pleasure" instead of something normal like "Nice talking to you." Way too formal. And then I actually shook his hand! Totally stilted. What a dweeb. No wonder he hasn't texted me back.*

Such second-guessing is like dropping one's tender heart into a tank of piranha. It's hard enough living certain experiences once firsthand, without having the self replay them ad nauseam later on.

18. The Self Suffers Scarcity

In the self's parlance, possessive pronouns abound: mine, yours, ours, theirs. The self likes to designate what belongs to whom, to demarcate its lawn from its neighbor's, our rights from theirs, his funds from hers. At root lies a scarcity mentality, a fear of not having enough. Such is our evolutionary heritage, an adaptive vigilance regarding resources.

The self's scarcity conditioning causes it to lose sight of the actual abundance that surrounds it. In Western markets, we face a dizzying array of options for all manner of items, from foodstuffs to clothing to home repair to health and hygiene to transportation. You name it and it has already been branded, manifold. Never have so many products existed that are designed for the maintenance and comfort of the human life cycle. Granted, not all people have access to such abundance; indeed, many still suffer deprivation of basic needs. However, at the level of survival and ballooning population, we can acknowledge that the human species as a whole has done well for itself.

The self's compulsion to inventory what belongs to it vs. to others causes the body-mind to contract and feel competitive. Perhaps you recall the experience of receiving the relatively smaller toy/serving/promotion/inheritance compared to another family member. Perhaps you noticed, as a result, a knot tightening in your stomach or the self's inner protest, its plan to restore justice and claim its due. A perception of lack constricts the heart, regardless of one's age. The self associates *acquiring* less than another with *feeling* less than another.

In contrast, recall the feeling that arose when you last shared something or gave something away. How did it feel to contribute that carefully prepared casserole to the potluck or pay for the bridge toll of the stranger in the sedan behind you? We haven't just inherited a scarcity/survival-of-the-fittest mind-set; evolution giveth as well, programming us with prosocial tendencies—voluntary helping behaviors toward offspring, extended family, and non-kin social groups. Even when it comes to money, research has found that spending an equivalent amount on another vs. on one's self results in more positive emotions and greater satisfaction.

Many clients have found relief from the self's scarcity fears by donating to others. One woman in her late seventies, struggling with depression and a limited budget and mobility, decided to volunteer at a senior center. Contributing her time and services elevated her mood and sense of purpose. It reminded her of the robust, plentiful inner resources she continued to have.

Altruism expands us. It helps us abide in a generosity of spirit that, we come to find, resides underneath the self's survival fears. Research has shown that before the self engages in its deliberations, a natural impulse toward sharing and cooperation arises. Once the scarcity self gets into the game, however, it requires extra proof and reassurance that shifting its possessive pronouns from "mine" to "yours" to "ours" will not result in a dangerous depletion of its reserves.

19. The Self Erodes

The self's abode, a thatched collection of thoughts and beliefs posturing as a stone-and-mortar villa, tends to wear down at the hand of the elements. The loss of a job or a relationship, for instance, can cause the self to question its foundation. It often must "reinvent" itself and reinvest in the masonry of its defenses.

Many people come into my office when confronting significant life changes, wondering who they are now that they no longer have a child at home to parent, no longer command the same earning potential, or no longer can access the same cognitive abilities. Entering into a new life stage such as retirement, for example, can rob the self of its identity as an employee or a professional or a wage earner. Without access to the underlying meaning and security of certain core roles, the self destabilizes.

Confronting changing roles and capacities is a poignant part of our humanity. It often requires reflection, support, time for working through a range of emotions. This is especially true for those changes mandated by circumstances beyond our control, such as having to adjust to the limitations that can result from accidents or illness. But the self often complicates the process of adjustment by resisting the current state of affairs. It may avoid directly processing the natural feelings of loss and grief that are essential in allowing one to integrate such a life-altering event and to eventually move forward.

The self's premise that it stands walled off from what occurs outside its house of mental activity is simply naïve. Life is a weathering agent and will erode false stories about who one is. Here are some examples of such self-stories: *I shouldn't be affected by the layoff; I should be stronger than this. I will continue to be a centerpiece in the lives of my adult children. I will always be physically fit and self-sufficient.*

These assumptions leave the self baffled and offended each time reality doesn't comply with them: *How dare this hip replacement interfere with my plans? Why isn't my son calling me on Sundays—what's wrong with him, with me?* In response, the self keeps engaging in infrastructure maintenance, trying to prop up its original scaffolding: *If I just stretch more, my body will be as good as new. My son always was selfish.*

The thought forms the self produces are like Jenga blocks, precarious towers ready to collapse. As all frameworks and furnishings eventually erode, the self would do better to align with something more enduring—like the open space under its roof.

What does that mean, practically speaking?

Just consider what doesn't have to change, what you have some control over. Consider, for example, the manner in which you engage with the changing structures of your life. Do you approach the challenges and blessings of each day, for instance, with curiosity, understanding, humility? Or do you approach them defensively? For, while we cannot halt the attrition of forms—structures, beliefs, bodies—we can preserve a gracious presence of being through such erosion.

20.   The Self Dies

Yes, everything dies. The self is not unique in this regard. But, remember, the self is not the body-mind; it does not die the body-mind's death. The self dies way before then, multiple times.

What?!

Okay, let's unpack that. First, let's consider the self's imaginings of death: the images, scenarios, worries about death that take up no small amount of thought. These fear-based reflections on the body's death tend to hijack the nervous system into a state of alarm. Just thinking about something does not make it imminent, but the primitive amygdala in the midbrain does not always know the difference. A fear-charged thought of one's death can activate a physical sense of threat, with all the associated fight-flight-freeze symptoms.

Perhaps you've noticed a high level of stress prior to a surgical procedure or when anticipating medical test results. Before a prognosis or even a diagnosis is given, the mind often jumps ahead to its worst imaginings, visualizing the doctor's grim face as she delivers the unfortunate news. In a split second, the self then jumps ahead to the painful, drawn-out, and, alas, unsuccessful course of treatment. Next, the wrenching bedside good-byes. Suddenly, there's a funeral and tears, regrets and unresolved grievances with family members who aren't delivering the kind of eulogy they should and...well, you get the idea. It doesn't take much for the self to play out its own death like a movie on the screen of the mind, spiking cortisol levels in the process.

As producer, projector, and audience of this death film, the self is quite stimulated by the (re)viewing of it. It's moved by the existential overtones—the questioning of life, death, the meaning therein. It feels compassion for the characters as they confront their mortality and sorrow. It experiences a base thrill in the gratuitous grisly details. The self, paradoxically, becomes enlivened by the virtual experience of its own death. Having the power to imagine its passing makes the self feel strong, immortal.

Not only does the self repeatedly kill off the body-mind figuratively, but the self also dies—quite literally—multiple times each minute! Every time the self-referencing operations of the brain are not activated, the self expires. As you may recall, the self is a process, not an entity. When the function of thinking about oneself is no longer turned on, the self—the language-based narrative of oneself—ceases to exist. But, from the point of view of this word-dependent self, such elimination is terrifying. The self generates as much ongoing self-referencing thought—"me," "myself," "I"—as it can to avoid this fate.

The actual lived experience of the self's death is fortunately benign and seamless. When you read a book, the self naturally fades out. When your attention is focused on a compelling play or television show, the self's inner commentary quiets. When you play an instrument, the self vanishes (if you're lucky enough to not have it re-intrude as an inner critic). No dramatic death scene. Just a harmless silencing that usually occurs without dread or detection.

And the story doesn't end there. Like *The Return of the Living Dead*, The Sequel, Part 5, the self comes back...again...and again. Self-referencing thought resumes with the "I" determined to pick up where it left off, to continue the chronicle of *its* life. The self does the quick work of patching up its narrative to either deny its ceasing outright (*I was there the whole time—in charge of everything that happened during that recital, that swim class, that nap, that coma*) or to minimize its blackout as a momentary lapse, a blip on its otherwise continuous, autonomous, undying operations.

The self doesn't want to acknowledge the ebb and flow of selfing that occurs without its consent. For if it did, the self would also have to acknowledge that its very existence lies at the mercy of some other, more primary source.

No-Self Speaks

The self tries so hard. Like the wooden boy Pinocchio, this fictional entity passionately wants to become a living soul. With its many self-hoods, this long-nosed puppet is desperate to become the real you.

But as we're compassionately drawn toward the self's plight, let's also be mindful of how much of the conversation the poor self has already commanded—within this book, within our heads, within our culture. It's time, perhaps, to focus on something else. Some One else.

Let's return to the question we asked at the beginning of the book: *What are we, if not a self? What's the alternative?*

Part 2 explores this question and the compelling features of what you are beneath the self's veil. In fact, the chapters in this section are written directly from the point of view of that source, the voice of the one who already knows you intimately.

Whose voice?

By way of answering that, I will just offer the keyboard to it now so it can introduce itself to you directly. Here goes…

Are you ready to present yourself?

Yes, thank you.

What a privilege to have the floor and the full attention of your readers. Usually I'm the last thing to get noticed. The *very* last. People tend to overlook me until the final moments of their lives, if at all. On their deathbed, they might just take a brief glimpse of me as the self's pretenses fade.

Don't get me wrong—I'm not complaining. It's kind of set up that way. To get to the naked truth of me, you have to peel off many layers—take off all of the self's clothing, so to speak. And most people like to keep their clothes on.

But let me step back a moment. I would like to formally introduce myself, though it's a bit ironic to do so as, well, I am...you! What you *really* are. Underneath the self's costume. I am your bare existence.

Feel free to call me no-self. No capitalization needed. Where I'm concerned, there are no personal pronouns. There's nothing personal about me at all, as I'm part and parcel of everything. But more on that later.

I recognize that no-self may not seem the sexiest of names, to be sure. I can understand that, after experiencing the humbling disillusionment of the self in part 1, you might like to come away with something positive or tangible to identify with from part 2. On the surface of things, no-self may appear an unlikely hero.

Indeed, in this section, as you step beyond the mirage of self and into the unknown expanse of no-self, skepticism may certainly arise. But rest assured, you will not be reduced to an existential blank. The spacious slate of no-self is not about your absence, but about your very presence. Your unfaltering potential. Come, let me show you...

21. No-Self: The Biggest Bang

I, no-self, realize that most people tend to want a larger, not a smaller, self. And they certainly don't want a zero, nonexistent self!

Paradoxically, I am just what the *bigger* doctor ordered. Despite my label of negation, "no-self" actually signifies the largest scope of identity possible. The "no" refers to what your identity is *not*: it is not a limited, individual, separate entity encapsulated in a limited, individual, separate body. What it *is* is much bigger than that.

Imagine casting the widest net possible from where you stand in your own field of awareness, from your mind's eye. The net falls across your whole interior: all your thoughts and feelings and bodily sensations and objects of perception. The net also falls over the entire environment that surrounds you—the chair you're sitting on, the street outside, your neighbor walking down the street, the neighborhood as a whole. All of these "outside" forms are also registered as objects of perception within your field of awareness. Everything you perceive as happening within you and outside of you arises within your experience of consciousness.

But this net is not only comprised of your exclusive consciousness. The net includes everyone else's consciousness, too—for it is all of the same one substance: awareness. The field of awareness, which here we call no-self, has no borders. It leaves nothing out. Unlike the self, the infinite field of no-self is not an *idea* of you that resides in your head. No-self comprises the universal substance and expression of everything.

In other words, I am the biggest you possible. With no-self, you're no longer a small self-fish in a big other-pond. You get to be the whole pond, the land around it, the life within it. You're the person dipping her feet into the pond, the duck floating upon it, the bird flying above it.

How do you know that this is yourself? Because it's all taking place simultaneously as the seamless content and context of your awareness. It's only through cultural conditioning that we've learned to divide consciousness into segments and assume it to be sourced within our individual body-minds. Scientists continue, unsuccessfully, to attempt to reduce the mystery of consciousness to a byproduct of the material brain.

If this makes your head ache—to claim yourself as the expanse of sky when you and everyone around you has been trained to identify as an insignificant wisp of cloud—then let it! For too long, the human mind has collapsed around narrow margins of corporeal personhood. This myopic lens has rendered the vastness beyond the body a muted backdrop.

I am no backdrop! No-self may appear as background to the self, the star actor in the spotlight. But no-self includes the actor, the stage, the rest of the cast, the audience, the walls and roof and all the empty space contained within and without the theater. I am simply the biggest (and only) show in town!

22.   No-Self: Fuel Efficient

To drive a self, one must be powered by a vast amount of fuel. The Mac truck of day-to-day functioning requires a constant supply of high-octane motivation. A reason to get out of bed. A goal to achieve. Something to look forward to. Something to prove. Something to avoid. A challenge to overcome. An income to earn. An education to achieve. A spouse to find. An existence to justify.

As a vehicle, the self is a gas guzzler, to be sure. Without a continual source of personal purpose, it would peter out. Selves need to feel successful, valued, in control, better than. They must be productive, liked, well-versed, accomplished. Even the fumes of fear are harnessed to push the self forward, the notion of failure being its own kind of petrol.

What fuels me, no-self?

I run clean and green, generating my own momentum. My drive is simply *life serving itself*. Initiative and action come forth from the unconditional creative ground of being. It's what consciousness is fundamentally compelled to do.

I am what naturally flows through you when the self gets out of the way. Think of your own experience. Do you really require a self-based pep talk each day to get up and take initiative? Without it, would you remain horizontal? It may sometimes feel as though the self needs to supply cheerleading for you to get out of bed, especially to counter its own negative commentary about the day ahead or how depressed it may be feeling. But, by and large, most people engage in feeding, conversation, and physical exertion without even thinking about it—that is, without being told to by the self.

This is because at the root of you lies *me*, no-self, generating life-sustaining movement. No formal declaration of purpose is required for this, just as people need not formally announce an intention to bathe, feed, or brush their teeth. Basic self-care continues on its own with no-self.

Basic other-care continues as well. As no-self, I do not distinguish between "self" and "other." An impulse arises toward the welfare of life beyond the apparent boundary of the individual body. When unimpeded by the self's survival fears, I tend to the care of the greater good, which happens to be quite healthful for the individual body as well. Just look at the physical and emotional benefits of such practices as altruism and volunteering.

Interdependence is hardwired at all levels—within neural networks, within relationships and communities, within ecosystems. Your interconnectedness as no-self moves you and all of life toward the remembrance and service of wholeness.

23.   No-Self: The Better Lover

Ever tried kissing someone who took themselves too seriously? Or what about you—ever lean self-consciously toward someone special, trying to direct each micro-movement toward contact like mission control counting down a shuttle launch?

Watch how self-commentary squashes the magic, how the self's analyzing pulverizes the chance for a truly spontaneous connection. When leaning toward a sensual encounter, we don't need to heed the neurotic, nattering ego.

Want intimacy? Then I, no-self, am the right one. No-self enables genuine connection with life. You get to *live* the raw emotional, physical contact of the moment. While the mind still generates thought, no-self doesn't identify exclusively with the inner commentary or permit it to drown out the visceral sense of the experience.

The relative stillness of no-self also allows for a startling recognition: that the consciousness within you is the same as that within the person you're looking at! It's the same pure light of awareness. And, if you look closely, it illuminates all other beings as well.

See for yourself. Allow yourself to look upon those around you with a softer lens. Specifically, release the self's judgments about those people. Try it now. Let go of the self's expectations about their usefulness, what they should be doing for you. Let go of the self's comparisons, the evaluating of them vis-à-vis how aligned they are with your views. If there are any other overlays that prevent having a fresh, clear vision of those around you, go ahead and remove them as well.

Now, look again and see people without filter, as lit by what remains. What do you observe? Do they not share the same root longings—for belonging, for purpose? Are they not subject to the same hindrances, the same confusion and fears sprouted from the same selfhoods? Do they not, simultaneously with those hindrances, confusion, and fears, express a vital wakefulness, a dynamic animation that keeps them poignantly committed to their human lives? Notice what emotions surface when you stand on this compassionate, common ground with the rest of humanity.

From this perspective, a spontaneous feeling of love often arises. A warmth, respect, or openheartedness emerges toward others, toward the shared sanctity that crosses barriers of individual difference.

This is a universal love. This is my vibe, the current of consciousness. It is what makes me, no-self, the quintessential equal-opportunity lover, intimate with all, *as* all.

24. No-Self, No Shoulding

I, no-self, don't *should* all over the street. Only selves do that—roaring at others on the road about who should be driving faster or slower or not at all. Across all settings, the self "shoulds" people who are not complying with its expectations.

When living as me, no-self, personal desires about "how things should be" do not get priority over the dictates of reality. Preferences about life continue to arise, of course. But they do not ignite a battle cry of "me vs. the other driver" or "me vs. the current conditions of the universe."

That doesn't mean, however, that one roams the streets as an indifferent zombie! When reality shows up as a six-lane highway suddenly narrowed down to two during rush hour, I acknowledge the impact. I register a possible spike in adrenaline in the body, a moment of physical discomfort. I call the office to inform them I will be late. I do not, however, argue with what's already taking place. Unlike the self, I do not protest life's refusal to ensure my comfort and convenience.

Think of the calm that's possible when not expending energy shoulding and resisting conditions as they are. The next time you encounter a situation that pushes your buttons, notice how the habit of your self tempts you to respond with opposition toward what's taking place. Notice the impulse to curse the driver or your boss under your breath, to badmouth your difficult neighbor or the opposite political party. Then, slow down. Pause. Inquire: *What would no-self do?*

This is the path of peaceable coexistence: you and the current circumstances can coexist without getting into an argument with one another. The trouble is that the self usually commands the driver's seat. It equates a stance of acceptance with one of capitulation or surrender and, thus, fears relaxing its resistance to the current situation.

As no-self, you recognize that acknowledging what already exists represents quite an empowered stand. With no-self, action (and activism) arises organically, if called for. It need not come from self-righteousness or a stance of embattlement, being at war with the current state of affairs. When you identify as no-self, you're not resigning yourself to passivity. You're just taking circumstances less personally. For, in the end, life generates more or less traffic when conditions allow; it's not always about you.

25. No-Self, No Calories

When the self dishes out personality, it does so like a pizza, a ready-made calorie bomb of saucy preferences and predilections, congealing habits, topped with an assortment of moods, beliefs, interests, and intentions—all baked upon the crust of personal temperament.

I, no-self, am comprised of similar ingredients, of course, but without the heavy caloric loading. Let me explain...

The self strings together ways of responding, thinking, and feeling into memory, creating a formal sense of personality, of "who I am." For example, let's assume that one experienced a high level of stress in early life. Let's say that, as a result, a tendency developed to be on the alert for challenges and to feel anxious much of the time. Perhaps a restlessness developed, a quickness of temper, a leaning toward cynicism or caution. These early personality developments remain alive in the self's autobiographical memory, creating an image of oneself as, perhaps, an anxious or high-strung kind of person.

Once the self has an image of its personality, it tends to bind to it. The self adheres to its personality pizza—its narrative of how it's been baked. In this example, the self takes on the narrative weight of defining itself as "stressed-out," even if in the present it hasn't been feeling or behaving in a particularly anxious way. To stay consistent, the self starts scanning for anxiety-producing stimuli in the environment that will provide confirming evidence for its pigeonholed, "high-strung" personality. The bottom line is that the self needs personality to be consistent and stable over time to perpetuate the fiction of itself as a consistent, stable entity. The self can't afford to bake a new pie.

What does this mean for me, no-self? Unlike the self, I am not weighed down by how personality played out yesterday or last year. I allow for the fact that personality is a dynamic structure, more fluid than fixed. When you identify with the great chef of the present moment, personality does not carry the loaded calories of a past personal narrative.

Can you feel the freedom of not being confined by how you (mis) behaved years ago? The freedom of not having to fit into the box of being a particular type of person? Patterns may still emerge over time, but rather than constraining you, they would just be a small part of an ever-evolving process of becoming. If you behaved selfishly in the past, it would not be stamped on your forehead; you would not necessarily be destined to behave selfishly tomorrow.

Instead, I, no-self, express myself spontaneously through the body-mind right now, in step with the changing inner and outer landscape. I emerge, as it were, fresh out of the oven each moment.

26.   No-Self, No Judgment

The self wears not just the one proverbial rose-colored pair of glasses on its nose, but many spectacles of judgment through which it views the world. Each pair offers its own perspective. One set of lenses scans the environment, asking *What is not going well for me here?* Another provides a frame of comparison: *Who is prettier or stronger or better than me?* Another pair narrows the field of vision to *Who is in my way?* The self will wear as many pairs of glasses as there are selfhoods to defend.

To take off these glasses is to see the world without filters, as I do. As no-self, I have no illusions to protect, no predetermined view of whom I need to be or how the world should look. In being composed of the inclusive *isness* of consciousness, I am able to behold the suchness of things as they are. Nothing is left out.

Without donning the shades of judgment, the world appears fully lit. That is not to say that it's necessarily sunny. Everything is just plainly visible: acts of impatience and unkindness, cut-corners at work, the disease-ridden cat, the drought. These are all quite as apparent as the indescribable complexity of the daddy longlegs on the wall, the extraordinary machinery at one's fingertips, the courage behind an apology.

Nothing in my field of vision has to be excused or judged. But having no judgment does not rule out having preferences. I may choose to spend time with some people as opposed to others. I may choose to engage in certain occupations as opposed to others. Clear, neutral seeing does not mean perceiving the world as a bland wash of sameness. The same underlying consciousness lights all experience, but that's where the sameness ends.

No-self is about living in a spaciousness that is fully inclusive. What is that like? Most people already have had the experience of such spaciousness (from self) when in nature. Natural landscapes tend to be encountered on their own terms without the mind's filmy analysis. Can you recall the experience of walking in the woods, seeing the foliage as it is, without expectation of order among the trees, without judgment against the aging branches relative to the newer limbs, without a mental filter of how it should look?

Imagine if you partook of the same clean perspective upon waking in the morning, turning with fresh eyes to the being lying beside you, to the relative on the phone, or to the checkout clerk at the grocery store? What would be revealed if you took off the thick lens of *How is this person meeting my expectations?*—or, more likely, perhaps, *How hasn't this person met my expectations?* Imagine encountering the daily commute without the filter of it as *an imposition*. Or walking into the office with 20/20 vision of the staff as they are rather than as an extension of the self and its need to get things done.

Living without a self that references everything back to itself allows for a 360-degree view. I, no-self, am thus the consummate transparent eyeball, as the romantics might say, receiving the world without glasses to shade or shadow it in judgment.

27. No-Self, No Time to Lose

The self often frets about not having enough time. It regards time as a limited resource and obsesses about the need to save it. Ironically, this costs the self a great deal of time, psychologically speaking, with all the worry spent on *getting there faster, being more productive, not wasting precious minutes*.

But from where I stand, time doesn't exist. As no-self, you realize that time is more of an impression than an actual thing. One can have a sense of time, but not the object itself. When did you last possess— that is, hold in your hands—hours off the clock?

Here's what creates the all-too-compelling sense of time: the self either props up the corpse of the past in its memory banks, or the self projects an image of the imagined future against the screen of the mind. Without such machinations of mind and memory, past and future time zones don't really exist as accessible locations.

Unlike the self, I do not slog a linear trajectory from the past to the present to the future. I do not scale a time line that tries to get to a forecast that is forever out of reach.

I, no-self, am seated, instead, in the large, luxurious chair of the present moment—for this is the only time zone one can ever truly participate in. The Now is not a concession prize to the future. The present moment is the real deal, an ever-presence that never runs out.

28. No-Self, No Tests

Tired of tests? I'm not talking about math quizzes or spelling bees, but rather the endless relational tests that selves deal out to each other. These are the trials the self purposely, if unconsciously, puts other people through in order to determine whether they will be accepting, available, or compatible enough.

Such tests can be subtle: *I'll wait for her to call me first,* or *Will he even notice if I don't say a word?* Or the tests can be quite dramatic, making and breaking relationships: *I'll give them one more chance to arrive on time,* or *If she doesn't apologize when I share my hurt feelings, I can't trust her as a friend.* The self tends to conduct these tests secretly, never letting others in on the fact that their behavior is being examined and the relationship graded accordingly.

When you identify as no-self, you never have to test another person again. The testing of people becomes obsolete as a defense mechanism because there's nothing you have to defend. When you start from a position of being enough from the outset, of already *being* love, then you don't need to keep collecting data to reassure you that others will respond to you in an affirming way.

Think of all the mental acrobatics—the mind reading, the misunderstandings, the subterfuge. You will be spared all that when you no longer have to put others through the self's tryouts. This doesn't mean that recognition of no-self results in everyone necessarily getting along. It also doesn't mean that you are blindly naïve and give everyone the benefit of the doubt, especially if there's been a history of mistreatment. But it does mean that, when you identify with your spaciousness, you're less likely to feel as wounded or to remain feeling wounded if someone behaves in a hurtful manner.

No-self rests upon a baseline of trust, not toward those who've passed tests, but toward the fact that, should a moment of hurt or disappointment arise in a relationship, you will be able to confront it and survive it. Such trust stems from the knowing that, as no-self, you approach relationship already whole. This eliminates the need for creating endless hoops for others to jump through.

29. No-Self: Selfless Parenting

Though the self may go apoplectic conceding this point, its presence isn't actually required for parenting. Consider natural history. Way before there ever was a self (that is, before a capacity for language-based autobiographical narrative developed), animals procreated and raised their young. They still do. The neighborhood cat doesn't need an internal monologue referencing its own existence in order to nurse its umpteenth litter of kittens. Likewise, the giraffe on the savanna, the elephant, lion, antelope, zebra, and most every mammal is gifted with a hardwired, selfless drive to care for its offspring.

Primates, as an evolutionary bonus, have developed advanced neuroanatomical structures that allow them to sport self-awareness. A breakthrough survival advantage! In terms of parenting, such self-awareness serves as delicious icing on the cake—mostly. For while the self and its conscience can certainly enhance caregiving, its drives can also complicate the raising of one's young.

For example, when the self regards its offspring as an extension of itself, trouble happens. The self who projects its own unrealized ambitions of being in the NFL onto little Johnny may unknowingly pressure him, attempting to live through his accomplishments. Or the self who struggles with anxiety may protectively displace its worries upon its children, installing fears: *Just you be ready and wait for the next shoe to drop, 'cause it always does.*

Selves may personalize their children's vulnerabilities or difficulties. Little Sarah's learning challenges touch a nerve for the parent-self who may have grappled with undiagnosed dyslexia growing up. Little

Asher receives an overabundance of everything he asks for from his parents who were very poor during their own childhoods. Such well-intentioned but overcompensating, self-referential parenting can take a toll on an impressionable child's development.

In contrast, I, no-self, regard my dependents in a way best described by the poet Kahlil Gibran: "They are the sons and daughters of Life's longing for itself. They come through you but not from you, and though they are with you yet they belong not to you" (Gibran 1923, p. 17).

No-self parenting is parenting without the self at the helm. It's about taking responsibility for children's well-being without investing a sense of self in their setbacks and accomplishments. No-self parenting is about mindfully participating in the universal effort and delight of bringing up a being that may or may not embody one's individual values or lifestyle.

Selfless parenting need not be sacrificial parenting. And you don't have to be perfect, since there is no right way to be a parent. When parenting as no-self, one just becomes conscious of the absence of guarantees. The self's illusions of control can no longer provide comfort. Informed and intelligent parenting comes forth without the pretense of predicting a child's future.

To put it simply, no-self parenting allows for a transparent type of caregiving, cleansed of the self's personal motives that may not always be in children's best interest.

30. No-Self Tastes Better

Dine with me tonight and you won't have to be seated with the self and its rowdy entourage—the internalized voices and unmet emotional needs that usually crowd the table and drive consumption.

I, no-self, enjoy food firsthand. I experience the tastes and textures and smells without the interference of a story about past dietary misdeeds. I come to the table with a clean-plate, clean-slate approach, encountering the food in a fresh way.

You've probably already come into contact with such mindful eating if you've slowed down enough during a meal to appreciate the sensory experience that goes along with it. You may have noticed, for example, the delicate, ribbed shells of golden pasta in the bowl in front of you, before the self begins shoving them in by the forkful. Or the scent of sweetness and cinnamon of the banana bread before the self bypasses it with thoughts about the next piece of bread about to be eaten.

With me, thoughts come and go, but they do not drown out awareness of the persimmon's silky texture, the coffee's earthy warmth, the popcorn's light touch. I am fully available for savoring it all, including following the body's lead regarding appetite and satiation. Dinner does not have to be a battlefield: the self vs. the body.

As an integrated whole, no-self accepts the body-mind where it's at. Whether over- or underweight, whether modeling a fast metabolism or slow, I respond to the body's requirements in the moment without commentary. Detached from the self's blaming, shaming narrative, I offer a reality-based stance of acceptance that enables a wiser, more satisfying relationship with food.

So you won't find me diluting the gratification of each meal with a guilty conscience about past yo-yo dieting. I won't be flinging insults at a mature waistline. That behavior only comes from the self.

31. No-Self, No Lost or Found

Selves make a point of trying to "find" themselves. They go to remote places, engage in special rituals, and read self-help manuals seeking out who they are. It's as if the self seeks directions to the buried treasure of a (nonexistent) golden, singular self-core.

You do not need to search for me, no-self. You can neither lose me nor find me. After all, where would I go? I am all-inclusive, as much present on a mountaintop as in a library as in a bathroom stall. There's literally no place where your no-self is not present.

Look around—everything is an expression of you. The seemingly separate environment around you is still perceived through your senses and awareness; it is a reflection of your consciousness. There is no separation between the object next to you and your *knowing* of it.

Rather than trying to find me inside something—in the right activity or relationship or occupation—just recall that I am what gives expression to these things to begin with. You cannot extract me from the doing or the being. For example, as you sit here reading this, consider where you rest your sense of identity. The self would have you believe that it should be with the body-mind who's holding the book. No-self, however, is fundamentally woven into the reading process itself. The body and the book are included, too, as both are intrinsically involved in the experience. But no-self is best represented by the *ing* words—the action words. No-self is the dance of awareness as it moves from read*ing* a book to gett*ing* a snack to convers*ing* with a friend. Happenings and the awareness of them occur simultaneously. I am constantly revealed in the seamless comings and goings of occurrence.

In this way, you can never be without me. There can be no hide-and-seek from me as one is never without consciousness. For this reason, I tend to not get so lonely. I commune with my manifold manifestation continuously.

If you forget this point, that you're always with and of no-self, that's okay. Grace often takes whatever form needed to remind you of this. Such graceful reminders can include the longing you feel for others when you isolate yourself or the headache you feel when you get caught up buying into the self's rigid thoughts. The pangs of unnecessary stress and aloneness can serve as clues to help you remember the ever-present inclusivity of your no-self.

32.   No-Self, No Lack

I abide in abundance, a defining feature of consciousness. Asking "Is there enough love?" or "Is there enough creativity?" is like asking a body of water if it has enough hydrogen. It's already in the human makeup.

In being no-self, you get to access a collectivity that lacks for nothing.

Here's a way to think about it: Recall the last time you had fun with someone. Try to remember the feeling you had and the experience that was shared. Now, consider this: Was it their fun or your fun? Whose fun was it and who had more or less of it? Of course, these questions can't really be answered. Trying to differentiate your happiness from their happiness, viewing fun as a limited commodity, does not make much sense for shared experience.

Shared experience, which is basically all of experience, entails a collective space—a "we" space in which the boundaries between separation soften. People access each other's joy, anger, inspiration, and frustration because they do not belong to the individual. This is true even though most people believe these things to be solely generated from and within their own body-minds.

Not being limited to a separate consciousness comes with great benefits. You might envision no-self as a vast stockroom full of overflowing barrels. Everything you would like to feel—generosity, goodwill, hope, compassion, and so on—is stored in its own brimming barrel. You do not have to individually manufacture anything. It is already part of your reserves, although access to it may be blocked at times by the self and its conditioning. Barring that, the limitless stores are as much yours as they are everyone's; these stores are humanity's birthright.

It should be said that my vast stockroom holds other types of supplies as well. The resentment barrel overfloweth, as does the barrel full of impatience, and the one full of doubt. Stores of anger, competitiveness, and self-righteousness are stacked against the walls, along with all the seemingly appealing aspects of experience. Again, all these feelings, responses, and belief systems pre-exist. You can't fundamentally be devoid of any of the barrels, though the self's shenanigans might convince you otherwise.

But just because these barrels are there, doesn't mean you have to supply yourself from them. That part is up to you. I don't really care which barrels you pull from. No-thing will get depleted. And no one selection will define you. Digging into the barrel of animosity during a tumultuous moment does not lessen continued access to the stores of contrition or forgiveness. Body-minds get to sample the whole array. They then get to play out the repercussions accordingly, as there's also no lack of cause and effect within my universal stockroom.

33. No-Self, No Target

If you don't have a self, then you can't be a target. A target of what? Of anger, blame, criticism, others' projections. Of course, people may direct these things your way, but without a self to receive them, the arrow goes right through. There is no solid core to penetrate. The offending shot basically meets a mirror reflecting the aggressors' behavior back to them. Even so, you may still choose to stand aside, not wanting to be in the line of fire. But the point is, you're less vulnerable as no-self.

The same is true for other potential triggers. Take watching the news, for example. How many selves do you know these days who can watch it with equanimity? With accusations flying, belief systems clashing, turning on the news has become a recipe for acute body-mind activation. Think of how the self responds, with adrenaline flowing and heart rate increasing, to counter, debate, lament, and protest what it sees happening in the world.

Yes, countering wrongdoing is perfectly valid and necessary. I, too, care about what I see. And, though I do not personalize it nor impulsively react to it, I do respond. My response, though, comes not from fight-or-flight activation, but from a place of compassion for the pain suffered by numerous misguided manifestations of me. Imagine seeing multiple deep gashes in one of your limbs. You would tend to them, not attack them and inflict further pain onto the festering wounds. You might also address the root of the problem so other limbs would not get hurt in the future. But doing so effectively would not require rage.

As long as some expression of me remains in the dark about its no-self nature, struggle will likely unfold as a result. This has always been the case with the seemingly slow awakening of consciousness. So, when pockets of unconsciousness act out from their selfhoods, I do not lose my Zen. Instead, I empower the awakened parts of myself to begin healing the division.

34. No-Self, No Aging

The aging self tends to dread the passage of time, marking it by what the body-mind loses: memory, muscle tone, youthfulness. It tracks and tallies these losses and, in doing so, creates a loaded psychological sense of time that compounds whatever wear and tear may befall the physical form over the course of its seasons.

No-self, however, is refreshingly timeless. Simply put, I do not age.

Impossible? Consider: How old is the awareness that peers out through your eyes? I'm not talking here about the aging skin around your sockets. And I'm also not referring to the self, the inner narrator with its aging cognitive capacities. I'm talking instead about the pure consciousness behind the self, the part of you that is *doing* the looking before the self comments on what it is that's being looked at.

If this is difficult to differentiate, imagine the metaphor of a lamp. The bulb (self) ages, as does the shade (body) through which the light shines. But the electrical current, the light itself (no-self), does not. It arises from its own source every moment with the same potential for luminosity, regardless of whether a particular bulb has dimmed or burned out.

Check this out for yourself. Does the part of you that feels love actually age? Or what about the part of you that feels moved by watching a beautiful sunset, or that feels touched by witnessing or conducting an act of kindness? Does that part age?

Again, we're talking about the timeless *knowingness* of these experiences, not the self's interpretation of them (which most certainly does change over time with mood and maturity). The no-self awareness that animates you remains the same regardless of the chronological age of your body.

This is because I have only one age: the eternal present. Unlike the self, I do not sequence passing moments along a linear continuum and carry them around like a chain. I may don a compelling flesh-and-bone earthsuit, but please don't mistake my ever-presence for such a capricious, corporeal form.

Part 3

To Self or Not to Self?

Having heard from no-self in part 2, it's important to realize that we can speak from and *as* no-self whenever we choose to. But first, we must be aware of this choice.

To be clear, the choice isn't about *being* no-self. We live and breathe as no-self right now. It's what we already are. However, we can ignore our no-self nature, as the vast majority of us do. We can overlook it without even knowing that's what we're doing.

No-self doesn't mind. It's not going anywhere. Unlike the self, it does not require our belief in it or attention toward it to exist. As the ground of being that graciously supports the self's tread, no-self is exquisitely deferential and will patiently await our readiness to claim it. If you've read this book thus far and resonate with the suffering of selfing, then I suspect you might be feeling ready.

The final section of *The No-Self Help Book* explores this readiness to initiate a shift in consciousness. It addresses the implications of choosing where to rest one's sense of identity, whether to self or not to self. There are disadvantages to maintaining the self as status quo, as current epidemics of discontent, escapism, and stress demonstrate. However, from the self's point of view, there are also real risks in knowingly abiding as no-self, which can represent a radical, almost revolutionary stance in a culture of rampant selfing.

This next section will help you weigh the costs and benefits of selfing. It will help you decide, after putting this book down, whether to go back to default—that is, to downsizing yourself through the self's lens—or to open to the peaceful expanse of no-self that already animates you.

35. The Effectiveness Test

As the final pages approach and you begin to sort through your own conclusions about selfing, consider this: *How well has the separate self been working for you?*

Putting aside for a moment the essential question of what's true, let's turn our attention to the pragmatic issue of what's effective. How effective is the self in providing you with your desired quality of life? Here are some criteria to consider:

1. How much peace does my self afford me?

2. How satisfied is my self with its life?

3. How does my self behave when it doesn't get what it wants?

4. How much do I love or even like my self?

5. Is my self's love for me conditional?

6. Does my self ever believe that it has accomplished, produced, or acquired enough?

7. How much more personal growth does my self have to achieve?

8. Is my self waiting for something before it can be happy?

Take your time with these questions. Be honest. This is an important evaluation, a life inventory of the deepest nature. If, upon reflection, you aren't too satisfied with the answers, with the self's performance, do not fret. You have some options.

First, you could just try to better your self—help it become more peaceful, more loving, more accomplished, happier, complete. Perhaps you already have. Perhaps you've made use of the many trades and industries developed in the service of cultivating an improved self: the personal growth workshops, the life coaching sessions, the full course of analysis, the assertiveness training... So, how did it go?

A healthier self is what brings most people to my office for psychotherapy. And, indeed, healthier selves benefit everyone; they tend to live more intentional, productive lives. Healthier selves adapt well to cultural norms. They're more pleasant to be around.

And yet, as part 1 of this book describes, the self, by its very nature, cannot supply the life satisfaction it's expected to deliver. Just interview someone with a "bettered" self and see how satisfied they are.

A second option for how to respond to the self's potentially mediocre performance on the effectiveness test involves shifting focus away from self-improvement altogether. You can give yourself permission to no longer hold the self-puppet accountable for the merits of the human soul. No matter how well-fashioned it may be, the self is like a sieve, unable to hold very well such qualities as peace and contentment.

Ceasing one's servicing of the self creates an opportunity to experience what is present when not selfing. In the resulting stillness that emerges, no-self may be able to catch your attention. Should you then align with the elemental consciousness that you are, you can apply the effectiveness test to it, to no-self.

You may notice, though, that when a personal self is no longer the center of attention, most of the criteria in the list of questions above fail to make sense. No-self requires a rewrite of the effectiveness test, an overhaul of its assumptions. See below:

1. **How much peace does my self afford me?**

   Peace is not something handed out like a prize for good behavior. Why should peace be distributed at the self's prerogative? Peace is a by-product of not being at the mercy of the self's commentary. No-self *is* peace.

   Inquire: *How comfortable am I with abiding in peace?*

2. **How satisfied is my self with its life?**

   The self makes a false claim to owning a particular life. It then evaluates how agreeable or gratifying that life is for the individual body-mind. No-self does not partition life like personal property. No-self does not judge existence based on satisfaction at some arbitrary moment in time, as life is continually emerging and changing. Life is whole, like no-self.

   Inquire: *How does it feel to identify with life beyond the body-mind's boundaries?*

3. **How does my self behave when it doesn't get what it wants?**

   No-self holds no illusion that life should deliver what it wants. Unlike the entitled self, no-self understands that life operates on the largest cause-and-effect scale possible. Should the moment disappoint, no-self graciously holds it in a much larger context.

   Inquire: *How does it feel to not personalize disappointments?*

4. **How much do I love or even like my self?**

   This question is like asking the sky how much it likes a particular cloud. From no-self's point of view, all expressions of itself, including all body-minds, are of the same essence—the same awareness. That essence itself could be described as love. All of no-self is comprised of love equally. Would we say we loved our left leg more than our right?

   Inquire: *Rather than wanting to be loved, how is it to be love?*

5. **Is my self's love for me conditional?**

   Again, this is a moot point with no-self. There is no separation between no-self and a "me." No-self and its love are of one continuous piece. You can't put conditions on what you *are*. (You can only forget that you are that!)

   Again, inquire: *Rather than wanting to be loved, how is it to be love, unconditionally?*

6. **Does my self ever believe that it has accomplished, produced, or acquired enough?**

   Being all-inclusive, no-self doesn't use yardsticks. It acknowledges that body-minds and their endeavors are processes that unfold at their own rates. Attributing value judgments to relative outcomes, such as what is "enough" at a given moment in time, does not make sense.

   Inquire: *How does it feel to be "enough" already, allowing for the emergence of accomplishment and productivity at its own pace?*

7. **How much more personal growth does my self have to achieve?**

   From no-self's point of view, there is nothing personal about growth. All of life is developing and growing. No-self doesn't hold an agenda for the rate or final fruition of this growth, as there is no end point to consciousness's expanse. No-self can relax and enjoy the evolving process of getting to know itself as it continues to emerge.

   Inquire: *How does it feel to experience growth not as a gauge for self-worth, but as an expression of ongoing intimacy with life?*

8. **Is my self waiting for something before it can be happy?**

   No-self doesn't withhold anything from itself. When happiness arises, no-self is there to meet it. There are no prerequisites, such as having to have a certain relationship, a certain amount of money, or a certain degree of cooperation from the body. As each emotion comes and goes on its own, no-self experiences it without filter or condition.

   Inquire: *How does happiness feel when it arises? What is it like to experience emotion cleanly—without the self's story about what should or shouldn't be felt?*

When applying the effectiveness test to no-self, we must remember that effectiveness is a conceptual yardstick designed by the self for evaluating "its" life and its job living it. From no-self's inclusive view, effectiveness is an empty concept. Like the acorn before the oak, the expression of consciousness continues to be both complete and evolving, with each moment comprehensive in and of itself.

36. Acting *As If*

For those fully identified with the self, no-self might appear to be a foreign concept or alien reality (landing in your hands in the form of this preposterous yet strangely compelling book). But, as we've discussed and as countless mystics, sages, philosophers, and even scientists have detailed, no-self is no concept. It is not an idea or theory. It occurs altogether independent of our thinking process or of our belief in it.

Even so, no-self tends to be approached, if at all, at arm's length—intellectually. A true experiential immersion as no-self, while accessible to each and every person, is another matter.

So to begin exploring the disadvantages and advantages of no-self *now*, without having to wait for the grace of a visceral comprehension or "grokking" of it, we can call upon the power of our imagination for assistance. The acting *as if* method can be helpful in providing a path toward remembering and coming into relation with no-self. Lest you think of this disparagingly as just "pretending" or "fake it until you make it," consider what pretending actually entails. The word "pretend" originates from the Latin: *prae* (pre) *tendere* (stretch), to stretch forth. Imagination stretches us forth, toward that which the rational mind may not be ready to envision or accept. It catalyzes our creativity or, more accurately, catalyzes us to manifest what our creativity makes possible.

The *as if* method, in brief, invites one to act as if one already has what one is looking for. For instance, when the self lacks confidence socially, it can operate as if it were competent or at least adequate interpersonally. This fantasy helps the self successfully navigate intimidating social situations and thus generates genuine skill and confidence that the self can integrate more fully later. Likewise, when the self believes that it is bad at heart (as many Western selves do, given indoctrination in the long tradition of original sin), it can behave as if it were good. Rather than walking around hating itself, the self is instructed to act as if it liked itself, allowing it to gradually come into contact with a genuine goodness of heart underneath its conditioned negative self-talk.

Usually, a shift in mood results when a positive outlook is engaged, even if one initially feels as though one is acting. I do hesitate, though, to assign this practice to clients too often, as I've found that substituting one set of thoughts for another only goes so far. The preferred thoughts may end up taking root as new, healthier beliefs, but the self is a fundamentally inadequate construct to begin with, as this book discusses. Thus, there is only so much mileage to be squeezed out of self-related thoughts, no matter how positive. A more transformative approach is to examine how all thoughts and beliefs are arbitrary concepts of mind, too unpredictable to inject with personal identity.

Nevertheless, for present purposes, we can employ the *as if* method as a thought experiment, allowing us to begin imagining abidance as no-self. Such a taste of our true nature can whet the appetite for deeper no-self embodiment. Here are the instructions:

1. **Place aside the default assumption that you are what your self says you are.**

   If the self calls you stupid or smart, ambitious or lazy, nice or mean, kindly thank the self for its labels, but don't invest any credibility in them. Just return your attention to whatever activity you already happen to be doing, like reading this paragraph. You don't have to get the mind to stop generating thoughts. (That's impossible.) All you need to do is to refrain from *believing* the thoughts. When the mind generates its most sticky convincing thoughts, treating you as though you were a limited, material body separate from all the rest of creation, you can politely tune it out the way you would a television program that you're not interested in.

2. **Begin acting as if you were, instead, the awareness that animates you.**

Notice the awareness that is looking out through your eyes right now. Notice how it doesn't have any labels attached to it, how it's just a neutral, observant field of knowingness. Notice how it never leaves you, how the witnessing of your experience never falters, no matter what thoughts, if any, the mind happens to be churning out. Begin identifying as that awareness.

3. **Begin acting as if all the physical sensations, emotions, and mental thoughts that you experience are just fleeting fragments passing through this same awareness.**

Employ the image of the sky here. The sky (the vast consciousness of you) happens to host the passing bodies of clouds (your thoughts, feelings, sensations). These vaporous forms are a small expression of the sky but are clearly not the sky itself. The no-self sky holds everything within it, but it is vastly more than its transient contents.

4. **Begin acting as if this you-awareness were the same awareness that animates all life around you.**

   Continuing with the sky metaphor, notice that all weather in the sky is essentially made of the same thing. Though different fronts may move in (people, objects, settings, and occurrences in your life), the sky (awareness, no-self) is unaltered. It maintains the same generative space for everyone and everything. There's no division, no separate patch of blue sky for each being.

5. **Begin acting as if you were, therefore, interconnected with everything, as if the boundary that defined you was infinite and not a boundary at all.**

   Sky is sky. Everything in this vastness essentially shares the same underlying composition. You still get to be your own cloud or weather front, but you also gain a knowing that, in essence, you are the larger context. You recognize that keeping yourself separate from other parts of the sky is fruitless, an artifact of the mind. You begin to understand that bounded individuality is illusion.

6. **As you proceed with your daily tasks and routines, notice how it feels to act as if you are this oneness of no-self.**

   Notice how, as no-self, you relate differently to your thinking, your moods, to what's happening in your body. Notice how you regard "apparent others"—that is, those who appear to be separate from you but really are not. Notice, as no-self, how it feels to be unbroken, complete. Observe the experience of participating in life *as* life, as an integral part of everything.

We've been socialized to see ourselves as separate trees in the forest rather than as the forest itself, as the cliché goes. While this acting *as if* method may feel contrived, when we envision standing larger than partitioned root, bark, or branch, it helps us to remember the wholeness that has been dis-membered artificially by the self. All that wholeness requires of us is a clarifying of vision, a recognition of the intact broader consciousness we already share.

So, stretch yourself. Try acting *as if.* To cross the threshold of no-self, you just need to be willing to gently lay down, like a fragile package, the idea of your self at the door.

37. Smart Selfing

The moment one realizes that the mind is a tool, one can then break free of the self's artifice. To be clear, "mind" refers to the thought-generating machine that spins out many images, ideas, and story lines, only one of which is the personal narrative called the "self." It's been a privilege for me to watch students and clients come to the realization that their thinking is a somewhat impersonal process. At first, though, there's skepticism: *Why would I separate myself from the workings of my own mind?!* But then, after some inquiry, the insight ripens—that one *has* a mind, an instrument of thought to be used at will. This contrasts with the common experience of being used as a tool *by* the mind.

In other words, selfing doesn't have to just happen to us. We get to choose when to engage with self, and when not to. And now that we know that there is a reliable, unconditional foundation of no-self underneath the self's operating system, we risk losing nothing by disengaging from the self when needed. Should the mind do its selfing dance, no-self will continue to shine through, its integrity undiminished.

The insight that the mind's self-story is an optional tool we can pick up or put down has profound implications—namely, that one no longer has to be at the mercy of the mind's whims, moods, and motives. Jane can see her depressive thoughts and not *be* the depression. Bill can watch the anxiety activate his nervous system without taking each anxious thought at face value. And suddenly, the problems that caused one to seek help—the "not-good-enough" beliefs, the "guilty-until-proven-innocent" judgments, the "what-if" worries—have lost their charge. They may still arise in thought, especially if the mind has been conditioned to think in a certain way. But the products and habits of the mental apparatus are no longer conflated with who one *is*.

So, how does this realization change our day-to-day lives? It gives us the power of choice, placing us in the driver's seat of deciding when to act from our self-story and when to redirect our attention back toward our no-self nature. A variety of factors determine whether it makes sense to self at a given moment. A few key questions (in italics) will help you sort through them, as discussed below.

Waking Up

Waking up happens on its own; the self doesn't orchestrate it. But once awake, the self can hit the ground running—with a commentary about how you slept, how you're feeling, the day ahead, the day past, your entire future. So, do you engage with the self's narrative? Well, ask yourself: *Is it helpful? Do these thoughts motivate, inspire, guide me? Do I need or want to be audience to the self as it's showing up right now?* If the answer is yes, then go for it. Continue with the train of thought.

If the answer is no, come back to no-self. What this looks like practically is allowing your field of awareness to widen beyond the thoughts pulling for your attention. You do not need to silence or eradicate the self. Why get into a conflict with an operating system? Just shift your attention so that the system operates at a low hum in the background of your field of awareness rather than commanding the spotlight in the foreground.

Coming back to no-self when the alarm rings is simply waking up and taking stock of what your senses tell you—how the bed feels, how the light looks streaming in through the curtains, the sounds of the squirrels on the roof, the smell of unrefreshed kitty litter wafting in from the bathroom. It's being present with what's there without analysis, without engaging in the commentary the self dishes out the moment you open your eyes.

Eating Meals

When you're making breakfast, lunch, or dinner, do you want to waltz with the self? Again, to answer this, you may need to look at the particular thoughts in question. If the mind, for example, is gently reminding you of culinary hazards in the service of ensuring a better oatmeal outcome, you may choose to pay attention. If the mind is raking you over the coals for not having gone grocery shopping, for eating too much the night before, or ruminating on how long it will be before someone else will clean the dishes in the sink for goodness' sake, then maybe you'd prefer to redirect your attention away from that realm of thought.

Coming back to no-self while eating would simply be coming back to the meal—how it looks, tastes, smells. No-self is basically resting in everything consciousness takes note of, including but not limited to thought content. Check it out: *How does it feel to eat without having to give the bulk of your attention over to mind-chatter?*

If you're rushed and feel that eating for its own sake is a luxury you can't afford, you can always return to the self's multitasking—gulping down your food while making to-do lists in your head or reviewing your grievances toward your internalized stepmother for the nth time.

If you're ambivalent about where to rest your attention, just notice how it feels to shift your attention back and forth into and out of selfing. The most important takeaway here is the knowledge that you have options: you can return to the self/no-self crossroads anytime you like.

Being at School or Work

When you arrive at the classroom, workroom, boardroom, what is your self telling you? The gold standard question to ask is *Is it helpful?* This can also be directed toward your overall attitude, as selfing includes not only the sentences streaming through your head but also the conditioned outlook or emotional reaction that arises. For instance, as you sit down to the lecture in economics class, is your self prepping you to *just get through it*? When walking into the staff meeting, is your self's attitude a heel-dragging, eye-rolling *been there, done that*? Such anticipatory irritation, boredom, or dread is also an expression of self—a narrative projection of what the future will entail based upon how the past has played out. If you check in with your self and find that it's biasing you toward the present experience before it has a chance to even take place, you might want to redirect toward no-self.

No-self at school or at work is the equivalent of a clean slate. It's a relaxing into what the Zen tradition calls "beginner's mind," a phrase translated from the Japanese word *shoshin*, meaning an eagerness and openness toward experience; meeting it without preconception. A curiosity accompanies no-self into each unfolding moment, a wide capacity to receive the human common core exactly as it presents itself.

No-self will not make a tedious seminar on estate tax or a grueling performance review with your nit-picking boss other than it is. But it will allow for you to encounter it *as it is*—without the self's commentary complicating the experience with an additional layer of resistance, reactivity, denial, avoidance, or what have you. And you might find that, without that extra layer, life can surprise you by not conforming to your expectations.

Transitions

Transitions are the times in between activities, such as standing in line, driving home, waiting for an appointment to begin. The mind tends to be quite chatty during transitions. When selfing occurs, the invitation, yet again, is to check in with the content and inquire: *Does it add to my life right now?* If you're reminiscing about your last beach vacation while you wait for the colonoscopy and it feels like a comforting escape of mind, by all means, carry on. If, instead, your thoughts have you suddenly diagnosed with colon cancer just like your neighbor was last year—who died, by the way—and you find your blood pressure rising, maybe it'd be helpful to visit no-self.

No-self won't dispute such thoughts. Nor is it a guarantee of any sort in terms of preventing certain outcomes. No-self is just expanding your awareness to recognize *Mmm, here I am, waiting for this procedure with this flurry of thoughts and a knot in my stomach. And I'm breathing, and it's 3:30 in the afternoon, and that's a lovely piece of art on the wall in front of me, and that lady across from me looks a bit nervous, and I've gotten through unpleasant medical procedures before, and I'm feeling a little warm, I'll take my jacket off,* and *I smell coffee from somewhere,* and *my left toe itches…*

No-self is the largest context in which awareness of everything arises. The context does not necessarily express itself as a verbal stream, as exemplified here. (Words just happen to be the necessary currency of communication in this book.) No-self can present as a quiet, silent knowing of all the "ands" listed above. It is a recognition of your largest, most inclusive being, which has practical benefit in broadening one's perspective when transitioning toward what's to come.

Interactions

When we relate to others, a distinct personality comes forward. The self on the inside—the sense of who you are as your mind constructs it—can either facilitate the interaction between personalities or make it problematic. When on a date, for instance, the inner self may bring unnecessary attention to itself through such thoughts as *What impression am I making? What does she think of me?* If engaging those reflections in the midst of your date works for you, go ahead and answer the self's queries. If you'd prefer to focus, instead, on the conversation as it's unfolding and on getting to know the person in front of you, it might be helpful to come back to no-self.

The same is true for simple exchanges or pleasantries. Ask: *Where do I want to rest my attention?* Do you want to rest your attention on what's happening on the outside or on the inside—the "inside" being your commentary about what's happening? The answer may depend upon how constructive the commentary is. For example, does it feel constructive to review your personal history of humiliating social blunders as you say hello to your classroom crush and walk into the school dance?

In terms of interactions, the no-self option *is* the interaction. It's the connection with the (apparent) other as it's happening. Shifting to no-self enables full awareness of the moment—the range of feelings and ideas and physical responses that get generated during the interaction, as well as everything else that's not about the interaction. For example, when engaged in a tense exchange with someone, no-self maintains a breadth of observation—aware of the escalating tone of voice, the constriction of throat, the felt-urge to criticize the other or flee the room. While the self might be welded to externalizing thoughts (*How dare they… Why can't they…*), further activating the mind and body toward conflict, no-self holds the tension in equal measure with everything else that's true before, during, and after the interaction. It notices, for instance, the simultaneous continuation of breathing, one's enduring intelligence, the solid ground beneath one's feet, the vast skyscape, and so on. Thus, turning back to no-self when interpersonally triggered helps one remember that who one is, is much more than a person stuck in the crosshairs of conflict. Such remembrance will likely inform a different type of response to the situation.

Decision Making

To self or not to self when making a decision? Decisions vary. Straightforward ones, like deciding whether to pull off the road to get gasoline, won't necessarily activate self-referential thought. Compare this with choosing which job to apply for, in which personal reflection on one's interests and strengths makes sense. But watch out. When anxiety is present, there's greater susceptibility toward the slippery slope of unhelpful selfing: *I should have stayed longer at my last job. There must be something wrong with me for wanting to be a writer. What if I fail all the course work for nursing school?*

When decision-making thoughts become repetitive, demoralizing, and paralyzing, then it might be helpful to come back to no-self. No-self engages all the same capacities toward decision making without investing selfhood into them. For example, when contemplating a budget for monthly spending, no-self can engage the intellect and emotions in sorting through financial and lifestyle choices. No-self just won't take you down as it does so, because there's no "you" to become enmeshed with the budget decisions. A more or less frugal plan may get implemented, for example, without extrapolation about what that means about your worth as a person.

Downtime

Does selfing allow you to rest and recover from the day's demands—and to have fun? Check in with the content of your thoughts. Are your thoughts telling you to *buck up, be productive, stay busy*? Do you have to make a case with the self-arbitrator in your mind to have twenty minutes of playtime? Or is the self-talk understanding and supportive: *Of course you need to chill out after such a stressful day. Go ahead and read that magazine, play Plants vs. Zombies.*

If you feel conflicted about the whole notion of downtime, why not check in with no-self? No-self is the sum total of how your authentic being expresses itself in the moment. Sometimes that expression is not subtle: you stumble through the front door at the end of the workday, mentally and physically spent, too tired to properly operate the microwave to heat up a frozen pizza that would taste better baked in the oven but you don't have the bandwidth to wait that long. No-self's intuition about how to proceed with downtime often takes its cue from what's most obvious about how you feel.

***

We encounter these and many other opportunities throughout the day to slow down and make a conscious choice to remember who we are. This act challenges the cultural convention of automatically colluding with the self's unbridled assumptions: that the self exists beyond the mind's machinations and that it does so without alternative.

Smart selfing consists of engaging the mind's commentary in a deliberate way. After all, some self-talk may in fact be constructive, especially the "autocorrecting" kind, such as self-compassion or self-forgiveness. These narratives graciously take stock of the inherent learning curve we climb as individuals. Such is the self/no-self dance, the paradox of scaling, in our wholeness, the exhilarating slope of a very human curriculum.

38. Off the I-land

What happens when people begin to practice smart selfing? Let's address that by first looking at the status quo, at what happens when people don't. What has developed is a part-fantasy, part-reality sort of existence, a society where citizens reside much of the time in the netherworld of their own interiority, the mind's multiverse, preoccupied with etherlike images and words that drift by like apparitions. Though fundamentally interconnected with one another by nature, people's ephemeral thoughts have pronounced each of them an autonomous, separate "I." And so they inhabit the world believing they are essentially alone.

The reality component of this existence is forged when billions of fictional accounts of separateness collectively play off one another. Like a mirrored funhouse, these "I" reflections create a distorted conventional reality, a consensus of stark individuality. Everyone watches everyone else take their "I" stories literally. The "I's" are thus reinforced in prioritizing their internal mind-chatter and building psychological defenses to compensate for their aloneness. Each "I" tends to live on its own thought-based island, with its own resulting fears of inadequacy and preoccupation with securing enough materially, relationally, financially.

So, what happens when people start applying smart selfing? A psychological progression occurs from (1) automatic alignment with self to (2) dis-identification with mind to (3) discovery of no-self, and (4) eventual abidance as no-self. Of course, fluctuations occur; different degrees of reimmersion in thinking and not-so-smart selfing continue to cycle. But exclusive identification with the self becomes less likely the more one tastes the freedom of detachment from one's thoughts.

Sometimes a critical mass of painful mental content will push one over the threshold toward no-self. The feeling of being "sick and tired" of oneself can initiate a new manner of relating to one's mind. For some, detaching from the self's narrative takes place without suffering—for example, by following a thread of curiosity to a book such as this. But whatever the catalyst, the pivotal insight—that one's consciousness is larger than the thoughts it contains—is hard to shake once sampled.

So, perhaps, like the moth, we are not ultimately designed to keep a safe margin from no-self's flame. The moth seeks to merge with the light, its ultimate source, and, in doing so, to sacrifice its apparently separate existence. To know oneself as no-self is to willingly enter the flame and incinerate ego-bound wings.

Smart selfing acknowledges both the moth and the flame, the fantasy-reality play of form with one simultaneously being an "I" and a "we." Smart selfing prevents people from defaulting back to the self's solitary personhood. Smart selfing enables people to step off their I-lands and embrace being part of the One sea, trading a single piece of mind for encompassing peace of mind.

Smart selfing extends us. Significantly. The small self, with its stiff protective perimeter, is fundamentally incapable of being elastic enough to accommodate the grand expanse of consciousness. Claiming our largest no-self—which includes 7.3 billion humans as well as countless plant and animal organisms and the dynamic entirety of the planet itself—can be a bit, well, mind-blowing.

Recognizing this expanse of identity puts the trials and tribulations of our individual lives in a different light, one that the self may protest: *Here I am, trying to keep my family safe, earn a living, preserve my aging body, keep up with the next pad or pod or Internet upgrade—and now I'm being charged with assuming responsibility for all of humanity and the whole Earth to boot?!*

If the I-land–identified self should blow a fuse here, take heart: the individual psyche alone does not have to take on all the woes of the world. The life-consciousness animating you is the same source and expression of everything else around you. When you see past your body's boundaries to recognize the wounds and needs of multitudes as your own wounds and needs, you do so with the capacity to feel them and to face them. As no-self, one accesses an ability to respond (aka responsibility) from a place of life acting collectively on its own behalf.

If the self still grows intimidated and attempts to retreat back into its illusion of separation, gently inquire: *Where exactly shall I retreat to?* For, the truth is, you can't escape consciousness; you can only pretend that you're not it. There's no other primordial home to turn to.

39. The No-Self Revolution

Let's conduct a thought experiment. What if we were to do something radical like eliminate personal pronouns—"she," "he," "they," and the like—from our vocabulary? Words convey a certain perception of reality that quickly becomes reinforced the more we describe that view of reality or refer to it in our common speech. Changing our languaging offers us a way to understand the societal implications of no-self, of being fundamentally interconnected.

So, let's say we substituted a different kind of signifier, something neutral like a letter or two—maybe J or TJ, just for the sake of example. The main point here is that the new pronoun would not be a personal one—it wouldn't refer only to me or to you. Everyone would be referred to as TJ—your neighbor, the postal carrier, prison inmates, the president, your pets—*all* beings.

Okay, bear with this strange experiment just a little longer. Now imagine how this use of language would sound in different contexts, for example:

Instead of saying, "I injured my leg," one would say, "TJ injured its leg."

Instead of "She earns a lot of money," it'd be "TJ earns a lot of money."

Instead of "He hurt my feelings," it'd be "TJ hurt its feelings."

"That politician lied": "TJ lied."

"Your country is hostile": "TJ's country is hostile."

"Their health suffers": "TJ's health suffers."

"The forest is shrinking": "TJ is shrinking."

"My body is dying": "TJ's body is dying."

If we ignore the apparent absurdity of this shift in language for a moment, what hopefully comes through is a shift in outlook. We begin to see the universality of experience. We see that when others hurt, we hurt. We start to recognize that divisions—between people, countries, landscapes—are arbitrary. What affects one part, affects the whole. Without linguistically segmenting into separate selves, we come to recognize a shared participation and responsibility toward life. It becomes clear that there is no such thing as *my* life or *your* life. It's just life.

Just think of how differently decisions would be made if they were based upon such an understanding. If you really came to know, for instance, thy enemy as thyself—that is, recognizing your enemy actually *as* one and the same consciousness as you—how would you then choose to treat your "enemy"?

No-self awareness enables progression past a self-centric perspective; it is a means of bridging division with apparent others. After all, there's only so far the self can mature on its own, with its raison d'être to prove its separateness and self-sufficiency. Opening to no-self enables humanity to evolve beyond a psychological and spiritual adolescence of absorption with the I.

Humanity's prosocial proclivities could then fully come online. For example, "charity" would be seen as an automatic and humane giving to Oneself rather than a self-depleting donation to *others*. Local, national, and international organizations might not, as a result, have to perpetually scramble for funding to serve the greater good. Additionally, think of how recognition of such no-self unity might affect the recent trends of reduction in empathy and concerned perspective-taking toward others, how it might impact the current rise in traits of narcissism and materialism.

Other implications? If a country's citizenry really knew that all appearances were of the same oneness, it might not be as likely to marginalize portions of its population. In the same way, a no-self–informed society might expand indicators of domestic health beyond a single economic measure of the marketplace to focus on the whole. Growth might be measured, for example, in terms of gains in social equity, environmental sustainability, collective physical and mental well-being, not just GDP. After all, a physician wouldn't examine only one part of the body during a checkup: *Yes, doctor, my stomach is fine, but what about my lungs, kidneys, heart? Why are you not examining those areas?*

Smart selfing at the global level might begin to expose and address human elitism. It might enable, for instance, extension of legal protections of "personhood" to other entities. For example, the Whanganui River in New Zealand and the Ganges and Yamuna in India already have been officially granted the rights of personhood by those countries. Such fair and responsible inclusivity need not be utopian fantasy.

Such inclusivity also need not require the elimination of pronouns or "I" from our language, as Ayn Rand's fictional society does in her book *Anthem*. Smart selfing can engender an all-embracing worldview without sacrificing our individuality. With no-self, every being still continues to have its unique imprint upon the larger fabric of creation.

That said, with a no-self–literate culture, what emerges is more than the sum of the individual parts. Just as in jazz, where each performance is an improvisation that includes and transcends the contributions of the separate musicians, so it is with no-self. A communal intersubjectivity emerges from no-self consciousness that manifests an informed, creative, and beneficial intelligence. This intelligence blossoms as no-self becomes conscious of itself. The more people are able to get beyond their personal thought spheres and practice smart selfing, the larger the awakened field becomes.

This is how a change in cultural consciousness can occur. As a visual, picture an entire room full of people standing in the dark (of self-identification), holding unlit candles (unrealized no-self). It only takes one "locofoco"—a self-igniting match—to brighten the whole room. Each person only has to light one other person's candle for the luminosity to swell exponentially.

Then the momentum sets in. Like a social media wildfire, smart selfing spreads. More and more people experience resonance of no-self after beholding it in another's presence. Seeing beyond the veil of the self is no longer limited to a few select teachers and their followers. The center of gravity shifts. Exposure to one's largest identity, to TJ's largest identity, becomes accessible, normative, and utterly transformative.

40. The Homing Beacon

The No-Self Help Book invites you to come *home*, to get reacquainted with the unspeakable mystery of what you are underneath the self's story.

When selfing judiciously, as part 3 encourages you to do, one comes into contact with the call of no-self. Often beyond our conscious recognition, no-self tugs at us, summoning us to return and abide as our original, most inclusive nature. In this way, we are not so different from the salmon, compelled by an instinctual longing to trace the stream of our existence back to its source.

But, unlike the salmon, we do not need to wait until the very end of our life cycle to return to no-self, nor have the body die soon thereafter! We do not need to trek through treacherous waters or scale steep falls. We arrive home, not by journey, but by remembrance. No-self is already who we are, revealed when the efforting ceases and we no longer believe all the dictates of the self. It is not some esoteric process or unreachable destination.

What we do as no-self may appear to be the same on the outside as what we do as a self. Washing the car is still washing the car. But there is a difference on the inside. With the self, a self-conscious referencing of "me" divides the person from the activity. This does not occur with no-self; there is instead a seamless flow to experience. No-self is the undivided state, at one with form and activity.

While identifying with the self may appear more natural, allowing us to continue swimming downstream with the cultural current, do not be fooled. As part 1 of this book showed, having to maintain a wanting, needing, pretending, slicing-and-dicing, second-guessing, smirking, dominating, esteeming, whining, eroding, dying self is stressful. The self tends to engage with life as a struggle, a raging river that must be traversed.

Though most people who come to my office seek relief from this raging river, it is often difficult at first for them to even imagine an alternative. The self has invested so much in the "crossing" that the stillness of no-self, like an ocean at its depths, seems alien in comparison. Many assume the depths to be dull, anticlimactic: *What am I to think about if I don't keep worrying about my job performance, my health, my relationships? What do I talk about if I get along with my husband, my parents, myself?*

But once you begin to hold the self's narrative at arm's length, you find that what remains close at heart is not dull at all. As part 2 describes, no-self is not a washed-out spiritual bypass of life. You get to see and hear what else arises within you and around you when your thoughts no longer drown everything out. You begin to notice elements of goodness, beauty, and truth in people and situations that the self might not expect. A gut-level recognition of wholeness and wholesomeness begins to quench a soul-thirst the self could never slake.

One client described her dawning understanding this way: that, while the "bottomless well" of (the self's) longing and fears continued to get triggered, she could endure it by standing in the complete "fountain" of who she really was. Another client, who suffered childhood abuse and a resulting stance of "I hate people," gradually came to have compassion for the universal "fear that causes people to do bad things." Once her self began to feel safer, she was able to question the solitary identity she had defensively developed over the years and carefully move toward connection with others. A third client, after disengaging somewhat from her traumatic life narrative, described recognizing the same "love and trust" in the eyes of her dying father as in the eyes of her newborn son.

As discussed in this final section, you get to decide what approach will be effective in bringing you to peace of mind and to the identity you wish to embrace. Smarter selfing can help make you grace-prone, attuning you to the homing beacon that is no-self. If you choose to follow it, to accept the no-self invitation, your self won't vanish in the process (at least not without your consent). And you can always reconjure it whenever you want to.

So, really, what do you have to lose?

MeSearch

MeSearch brings together a sampling of research findings from studies on each chapter's core themes. Empirical and theoretical journal articles have been cited with the intention of whetting the appetite regarding recent inquiries into the nature of self and identity in the behavioral sciences, and the application of such inquiry for individual and collective well-being. This represents but a slice of an extensive and growing literature. I invite you to scan through the findings below and see which studies spark your curiosity.

1. The Imposter Self

In the late nineteenth century, William James differentiated one's mental self from physical self from spiritual self (James 1892). These concepts are replicated in contemporary neuroscience literature, with "core" or "minimal" self, "proto-self," and "autobiographical" or "narrative self" (Damasio 1999; Gallagher 2000; Gallagher and Frith 2003; Panksepp 2005). Researchers have additionally focused on features of the "spatial" self (Vogeley et al. 2004), the "social" self (Frith and Frith 2003), the "emotional" self (Fossati et al. 2004), the "verbal" self (Turk et al. 2003), among others.

Northoff and colleagues (2006) suggest a three-tier model of the self (sensory, experiential, higher-order cognitive) in which all levels are mediated by self-referential processing. In a review of neuroimaging studies, the authors find that the midline areas of the human cerebral cortex may be responsible for linking self-referential processing to different functional regions of the brain (such as emotional, spatial, and memory realms), and may thus be a potential "convergence zone" for diverse concepts of the self (p. 454). The degree to which a stimulus activates or relates to a subjective sense of self has been found to be associated with cortical midline structures of the brain (Northoff et al. 2011; Schneider et al. 2008; Northoff et al. 2006).

***

Rochat (2001, 2003), in reviewing the infant development literature, posits that self-awareness matures through five different levels from birth on, from implicit differentiation of self to explicit to meta-level self-awareness. Research has shown that infants come into the world with an innate, if rudimentary, ability to differentiate between self and other (as opposed to early theories suggesting a first state of fusion with the environment).

Self-awareness in a conceptual form appears to come online by eighteen months of age, corresponding with language acquisition and the ability to represent oneself symbolically. Such self-consciousness (i.e., the process of representing and describing ourselves to ourselves) is also enabled by toddlers' first awareness of their bodies (Courage et al. 2004). The capacity for body-consciousness enables children to form memories. These memories are soon elaborated with the emergence of language. Words not only enable communication with caregivers, but they also allow children to reflect on their own thoughts. In this way, the inner space of the mind becomes conceptualized and the subjective sense of self is born.

Children at four to five years of age are able to hold multifaceted representations of others and develop theory of mind (Rochat 2001). At this age, they also begin to know themselves by an interior narrative identity. Self-regulatory private speech (such as a young child mimicking parents' words in telling herself to "be careful" when walking down stairs) is associated with autobiographical memory development (Al-Namiah et al. 2012). The autobiographical story (Fivush 2011) continues to change throughout the life span (within the parameters of genetics and personality) with social and cultural conditioning (Marraffa and Paternoster 2016). The self is thus understood as an evolving, if precarious, construction (Marraffa 2013).

***

According to cognitive scientists, certain processes contribute to the subjective "I," such as sensorimotor and homeostatic operations that specify the self vs. not-self functionally, through perception, cognition, emotion, and action (Christoff et al. 2011). Studies have also found a self-referencing effect, such that information that pertains to one's self-concept is more likely to get encoded into memory and later recalled than information unrelated to one's self (Klein 2012).

***

On reviewing over two hundred fMRI studies, researchers have found that social cognition (understanding others' beliefs, behaviors, and personalities, and also understanding one's own personality) engages two parts of the brain (Overwalle 2008). The temporo-parietal junction activates when trying to infer temporary states, such as the intentions or desires of others. More enduring social knowledge, such as the norms or traits of oneself or others, gets represented in the medial prefrontal cortex, enabling reflection over time (Wagner et al. 2012).

***

The "imposter syndrome," first coined by researchers at Georgia State University in 1978 (Clance and Imes 1978), describes the tendency to attribute one's successes to luck rather than to skill, effort, or experience, as well as the tendency to personalize one's failures. The syndrome has been found not only among high-achieving individuals, but also quite broadly among a range of populations and professionals (e.g., Clark et al. 2014; McIntyre 2016).

Rough estimates have been made that 70 percent of the population has experienced imposter feelings at some point in their careers (Clark et al. 2014), but no empirical epidemiological studies have been conducted confirming this. Nor have empirical studies to date consistently found particularly strong evidence identifying clear environmental/personality risk factors in the syndrome's development (Sakulku 2011).

2. The Self Slices and Dices

Research on the mind's tendency to differentiate items into separate categories has demonstrated that people tend to categorize things based on prototyping—by how salient or central the item is relative to the category as they perceive it (e.g., Rosch 1973). This is in contrast to categorizing based on concrete definitions, with items meeting certain objective criteria. Results highlight the subjective nature of our most basic perceptions about the world around us.

Similarly, linguists such as Noam Chomsky (e.g., Chomsky 2000) argue that objects of thought are constructed (a compilation of mental operations) and are not independent representations of an external reality as such. Language provides a means of labeling our environment, for instance, but does so in a way that necessarily incorporates the mind's perspective on the environment.

***

Additional exploration into how words can shape thought and even affect material outcomes includes studies that show the influence of labels and names. For example, people have been found to prefer politicians with simpler names (Laham et al. 2012). When companies are given names that are easier to pronounce, their stocks perform better when initially listed on the exchange (Alter and Oppenheimer 2006). Results support a "fluency" theory, that people prefer information that can be easily processed, reminding us that language is not neutral. Rather, all labels are generated and received by the mind, influenced by its many concepts, images, and associations.

3. The Self Freezes

Different classes of repetitive thought have been identified and researched, including rumination, worry, perseverative cognition, cognitive and emotional processing, defensive pessimism, reflection, counterfactual thinking, mind wandering, habitual negative self-thinking, postevent rumination, and cognitive coping behaviors such as planning, rehearsal, and problem solving (Watkins 2008).

Watkins's extensive review (2008) of the research differentiates between constructive and unconstructive recurrent thought about one's self. Negative thought content about oneself is more likely to have unconstructive consequences (such as anxiety, depression, and worse overall mental health) than positive thought content. Worry thoughts that are abstract (about larger questions of meaning or self-evaluation) tend to be unconstructive as opposed to worry that is concrete (such as problem solving) in its construal. The consequences of repetitive thought were also found to vary depending upon the intrapersonal/situational context. A stressful situation, for example, coupled with lower self-efficacy or ability can result in unconstructive prolonged thought.

***

In a meta-analysis of studies on self-focused attention and affect, findings show that, overall, self-attention does correlate with negative mood and emotion (such as depression and anxiety), especially among women. Rumination was associated with stronger negative affect than simple self-focus. When self-attention follows a positive event or is directed on positive self-aspects, less negative affect is associated with it (Mor and Winquist 2002).

***

Thoughts constantly change. Cognitive science describes the concept of *mental motion*, the finding that thoughts have speed and variability that affect our psychological experience (Pronin and Jacobs 2008). Extremes of mental motion can cause problems, eliciting feelings of mania and grandiosity (Pronin et al. 2008) as well as biases that may compromise rational judgment (Kahneman 2011). Fast thought is also related to greater risk-taking behavior (Chandler 2012). At the other end of the continuum, reduced mental motion (repetitive, slow thinking) can cause negative feelings such as anxiety or depression, even if the content of such thoughts is not negative (Pronin and Jacobs 2008).

4. The Dictator Self

Neural differences have been found in the brain when people engage in internal self-talk that is monologic (involving a single speaker) vs. dialogic (involving conversations) (Alderson-Day et al. 2016). A widespread bilateral network of activation is associated with dialogic self-talk that corresponds, in part, with the networks implicated in theory of mind processing (the ability to understand that others have their own beliefs and feelings that may differ from one's own perspective).

Certain psychotherapy techniques (e.g., voice dialogue, Stone and Stone 1989) help identify different parts of the self—"selves" or subpersonalities—and engage them in conversation, shedding light on the many beliefs, roles, rules, and agendas at play within the psyche. This dialoguing helps integrate previously unconscious parts of the mind and prevents one prevailing or "primary" self from dominating psychological processes.

***

Significant differences have been found between using first-person pronouns (e.g., "I," "me") in self-talk during introspection and referring to oneself by one's name (as if speaking about oneself as a separate person) (Kross et al. 2014). *Not* using first-person pronouns enhances self-distancing and is associated with experiencing less distress when speaking in public and making first impressions, as well as with less dysfunctional postevent processing. Researchers found that when participants didn't use the first-person pronouns, they were able to appraise future stressful situations in less threatening terms.

Research on self-distancing and placing "self in context," as in third-wave behavior therapies, has shown that focusing on the self as an object of attention enables people to transcend an egocentric point of view (Kross 2009) and promotes better self-regulation and self-control (Fugita et al. 2006). Self-distancing is also helpful in enabling reflection on past painful experiences without rumination (Wisco and Nolen-Hoeksema 2011). For this reason, detaching from the self has been incorporated into forms of cognitive therapy, allowing people to gain better perspective and acceptance of their thoughts and feelings (Teasdale et al. 2002; Hayes et al. 2006).

***

One study investigated what leads people to locate their sense of self either in the heart or in their brain (Hajo et al. 2015). Those more inclined to locate the self in the brain included men, Americans, and people with a greater sense of themselves as independent. Women and those with more of an interdependent concept of themselves were inclined toward locating the self in the heart. Perceived location of the self was influential in terms of affecting participants' attitudes about controversial medical procedures (such as abortion and the legal definition of death). It also impacted the amount of effort and money participants were willing to invest in various charities.

5. The Self Seeks Esteem

Large-scale longitudinal studies have identified age-related trends in self-esteem, with lowest levels found among young adults, and highest levels peaking at age sixty and then declining, especially after retirement (Orth et al. 2010). High levels of self-esteem are found among children, dropping by adolescence, especially among girls (Robins et al. 2002). Higher income and better health later in life appear to maintain higher levels of self-esteem. People in supportive relationships also demonstrate higher self-esteem. The sharp drop in self-esteem later in life around age seventy may be related to role losses or physical deterioration. Or it may be indicative of less self-aggrandizement and self-promotion as one becomes wiser and more comfortable with who they are (Baltes and Mayer 1999).

***

Certain parts of the brain "light up" when we engage in self-evaluation and when we process feedback from others about ourselves (Yang et al. 2012). Feelings of self-worth have been found to correlate with the connectivity of the frontostriatal circuits in the brain. These neural systems link areas responsible for self-referential thoughts with those responsible for positive emotion and evaluation. Results of fMRI studies suggest that self-esteem thus arises from a "distributed brain network" rather than from the functioning of one singular region (Chavez and Heatherton 2014), emphasizing the process nature of *self-esteeming* (the process of trying to acquire adequate self-worth).

***

Self-esteem can affect how people integrate information about themselves. Those with high self-esteem are more able to respond to information that attributes positive qualities to the self. For people with low self-esteem, however, positive self-related information tends to create anxiety (Danielsson and Bengtsson 2016).

Researchers have also found that the self engages in self-serving biases in the face of self-threat—"adaptively" disengaging from negative feedback and outcomes as a way to preserve self-esteem (Leitner et al. 2014). For example, students high in academic self-esteem were more likely to engage in derogation of a task when they received negative feedback about their performance on it (Mackinnon 2015). Studies using fMRIs have even located the brain regions potentially responsible for such management of self-threat by way of self-enhancement (e.g., the anterior cingulate cortex) (Hoefler et al. 2015).

***

Studies have shown that when people base their self-esteem on external sources—such as other people's approval of them, their appearance, or their academic performance—they report more stress, anger, and eating disorder symptoms; more academic and relationship problems; and increased rates of alcohol and drug use (Crocker 2002). Those who source their self-worth from internal factors, such as being virtuous or abiding by a moral code, are less likely to develop problems with alcohol, drugs, or eating disorders. They are also more likely to get higher grades.

Research has shown that it may be better to praise children's efforts than their personal qualities (Brummelman et al. 2013). Children with low self-esteem who are praised for their qualities ("You're such a good athlete, student, artist," etc.) were found to experience more shame and even lowered self-esteem when they didn't do well on later tasks. Those who were praised on their efforts ("You really tried") did not experience shame or diminished self-worth following future failures.

***

The risks associated with self-esteeming include an association between *contingent self-esteem* (self-worth dependent upon others' feedback) with greater depressive symptoms and suicidal behavior (Lakey et al. 2014). Younger adults who are depressed report wanting boosts to their self-esteem and yet find they do not actually like the boosts (Bushman et al. 2012). Performance-based self-esteem has also been found to be a strong predictor of burnout over time for working men and women (Blom 2012). Self-esteem instability is associated with certain personality dimensions, such as low levels of emotional stability, agreeableness, and conscientiousness (Zeigler-Hill et al. 2015).

***

Neff (2011) proposes that self-esteem is not the cause but the outcome of healthy behaviors, such as mindfulness. Studies have found that mindfulness can increase self-worth and life satisfaction. Even brief inductions of mindfulness can increase state self-esteem (Pepping et al. 2013). Neff's research (2011) finds that, whereas self-esteem can be associated with narcissism, self-compassion is not. Self-compassion is associated with steadier self-worth than self-esteem, as it is not based on external contingencies.

6. The Self Wants

Scientists have found that wanting more negatively correlates with well-being. Wanting what one already has, on the other hand, makes well-being more likely (Ian and Larsen 2011), confirming the conventional wisdom that "happiness is not having what you want, but wanting what you have" (Schachtel 1954, p. 37). One study found that becoming less materialistic predicted improvements in well-being (Kasser et al. 2014).

Consumer goods have been found to function as a compensatory salve that reduces the distress caused by the gap between how one perceives oneself and how one desires to view oneself (Mandel et al. 2014). Addressing this gap by, for example, boosting feelings of worth among adolescents discourages materialistic values (Chaplin and John 2007).

Even when people acquire surplus material possessions or extreme wealth—such as through the winnings of a lottery, for example—they are no more likely to experience happiness than they were prior to their acquisitions (Brickman et al. 1978). The tendency has been labeled the *hedonic treadmill*, noting how the more you accumulate (money or otherwise), the more you end up desiring. This results in an ever-increasing treadmill pace toward the carrot of happiness (Brickman and Campbell 1971; Eysenck 1990).

***

Studies have demonstrated a relationship between self-esteem and the desire to self-enhance through the accumulation of material possessions (Park and John 2011). Uncertainty and self-doubt have also been linked to materialism (Chang and Arkin 2002). Connections have additionally been made between narcissism, materialism, and conspicuous consumption (Cisek et al. 2014).

***

Distinctions have been found between wanting something and liking it. When we become addicted to something (such as with alcoholism), instead of being motivated by liking the substance, we become motivated more by wanting/craving it. The incentive-sensitization theory proposes that wanting-motivation and liking-motivation are separable, associated with distinct brain mechanisms (Ostafin et al. 2010).

Hyperactivity of subcortical "wanting systems" has been tied to such addictive behaviors as drug use and gambling. Research finds that these same unconscious wanting processes drive our behavior in regular everyday instances such as when purchasing a product that one doesn't actually like (Anselme and Robinson 2016).

7. The Self *Needs*

Different theories have been proposed about the psychological needs that motivate human behavior and well-being. In a review of six different models of needs, researchers conclude that there is no one common set of basic human needs, although the need for relatedness, belonging, or affiliation does get mentioned across theories (Pittman and Zeigler 2007).

***

Self-determination theory posits that competence, autonomy, and psychological relatedness comprise innate, universal needs essential for psychological health (e.g., Ryan and Deci 2002). Self-determination theory views such needs as intrinsically motivated, activated for their own sake (vs. being activated in response to an external source or reward), reflecting an inherent drive toward stimulation and growth.

***

Maslow's hierarchy of needs proposes that people are driven by different levels of needs (depicted as a pyramid), with the bottom levels seen as prerequisites before the meeting of higher-order needs (Maslow 1943). This five-stage model includes, from the base up, physiological needs, safety needs, belongingness and love needs, esteem needs, and self-actualization (achieving one's full creative potential) needs. Maslow later added aesthetic, cognitive (Maslow 1970a), and transcendence needs (Maslow 1970b) into his model.

While Maslow's model contributes a significant holistic approach to understanding humans and their potential, his research methods have been called into question in terms of the representativeness of his sample population and the generalizability of his results. Contemporary research has found that, although certain tiers of needs do appear to be universal across all cultures, the most basic needs do not need to be fulfilled before getting benefit from the higher-order ones (Tay and Diener 2011).

***

Manfred Max Neef's taxonomy of fundamental human needs, human-scale development, defines needs in a matrix that includes categories of being, having, doing, and interacting that intersect with the following needs: subsistence, protection, affection, understanding, participation, leisure, creation, identity, and freedom (Max-Neef et al. 1989). This model has informed sustainable development, with regard to the planning of social institutions designed to meet such nonhierarchical needs.

***

Research has found that people of Generation Y (the "Millennials") score progressively higher in entitlement than the previous two generations (Laird et al. 2015). The researchers believe a higher inflation of self to be responsible (secondary to the "self-esteem movement"), which results in unrealistic expectations for this generation and chronic disappointment.

Research on entitlement in the workplace has found that psychological entitlement moderates the relationship between perceived letdowns by the organization and employee depressive mood states (Priesemuth and Taylor 2016).

8. The Self Whines

The power of whining to attract the attention of listeners has been studied empirically. Whining has been found to be even more distracting than infant cries, machine noise, or *motherese* (the speech patterns used by parents when speaking to very young children) (Chang and Thompson 2011). Participants in a memory study made more mistakes and had higher physiological activation when interrupted by whining than by other vocalizations. These results suggest an auditory sensitivity among humans to these vocalizations, possibly attachment-related (Chang and Thompson 2010).

***

The tendency to complain, like most behaviors, has been found to depend upon an individual's attitude toward complaining, personality traits (such as inclination to become dissatisfied), and situational factors such as the extent of loss/disappointment involved (Thorgersen et al. 2009). Adverse effects of chronic complaining have also been the subject of inquiry, especially the negative impact on mental and physical health. Monitoring self-talk and gratitude have been proposed to counter the habit of complaining (Cameron 2015).

***

A study of the personal dynamics at play in decision-making groups found a correlation between whining and bullying (Henningsen and Henningsen 2017). People tended to respond to bullying behavior with whining and submissive behavior. The presence of either bullying or whining was associated with perceptions of less decision-making effectiveness and less group cohesiveness. The researchers consider whining an aggressive tactic, a method of securing pity to get one's needs met.

***

A longitudinal study of preschool children found that those who demonstrated "whiny" attributes (inhibited, fearful, rigid, easily offended, indecisive, overcontrolled, easily victimized) were more likely at age twenty-three to exhibit relatively conservative political views with associated traditional gender-role beliefs and difficulty with ambiguity (Block and Block 2006). Preschoolers who demonstrated self-reliant, resilient, energetic, relationship-seeking, undercontrolled, and dominating characteristics were found to hold relatively liberal views two decades later with wide and nonconforming interests.

9. The Self Is Picky

Confidence in one's preferences has been studied, with researchers finding that people tend to be more confident each time they repeat the same choice. Each time they do so, they are also more likely to continue repeating that choice (Koriat 2012).

***

Research on attitudes (e.g., a person's favorable or unfavorable stance toward an object) in Western psychology has tended toward emphasizing the stable and consistent nature of the individual. A shift in attitude theory has been proposed, based upon non-Western sociological contexts, that regards attitude as context-specific, incorporative of the views of others and of social norms (rather than being person-centric and primarily reflecting the self's identity). This "normative-contextual model" theorizes attitudes to be less personal and more functional to the extent that they help one adjust to new contexts, valuing relational embeddedness as opposed to self-expression (Reimer et al. 2014).

An emphasis on normative preferences as opposed to personal preferences has been observed in non-Western cultures. One's agency is sourced, not from expressing one's preferences but from referencing what is best relative to others and to the situation (Trommsdorff 2009). Also, in non-Western cultures, principles of change, instability, and holism result in a greater tolerance for contradictions in attitudes or preferences. In Western culture, in contrast, people tend to emphasize intrapersonal consistency and what's "true" with regard to their attitudes; they are less accepting of duality or dialectic thinking (Nisbett 2003). Westerners have also been found to be more consistent over time in their preferences, especially when the target of their preference is something that aligns with their self-concept (Wilken et al. 2011).

***

Scientists examined observed similarities in couples and found a correlation between partners' body mass index, height, educational qualifications, and even blood pressure measurements. The study found that the couples not only resembled each other on the physical attributes, but also in terms of the region of the genome that underlies the attributes. The researchers conclude that there is a genetic basis for assortative mating (Robinson et al. 2017).

***

Sociological studies have shown a tripling over the past two decades in the number of people who claim that there is no one with whom they can talk to or confide in (McPherson et al. 2006). Researchers believe that the shrinking social networks are indicative of less connection to community and neighborhood.

10. The Self Smirks

The motivations behind social comparison vary, according to advances in research on social comparison theory. People who are trying to self-evaluate and simply know themselves better tend to pick comparison targets similar to themselves (Thorton and Arrowood 1966). Those who desire self-enhancement may engage in upward or downward social comparison, choosing people who are superior or worse off as a means of lowering or elevating self-regard (Tesser et al. 1988; Wood 1989). Studies have shown that those with low self-esteem tend to improve their mood by engaging in downward social comparison (Aspinwall and Taylor 1993). Other examples of social comparison motivators include self-improvement, self-assessment, and self-verification (Dauenbeimer et al. 2002).

***

Researchers have shown that people perceive facial expressions that onset differentially in the left vs. right half of the face as providing subtle signals about the person's spontaneity and genuineness. Inferences about a person's trustworthiness are affected by such lateralized facial expressions (Carr et al. 2014). Other studies have shown that when people are rejected, they are better at perceiving whether another's "happy" facial expression is genuine or deceptive (Bernstein et al. 2008). People fearing or facing rejection tend to be more sensitive to social cues.

Masking smiles, facial expressions that conceal negative emotions, have been studied. A smile that engages the upper lip corners and the orbit around the eye (called a Duchenne smile) has been found to engage different brain physiology and be correlated with a different subjective emotional experience than a smile that only pulls up the lips (a masking smile). The Duchenne smile is associated with genuine enjoyment and positive emotions (Ekman et al. 1990).

Researchers have found that people who display more genuine Duchenne smiles (vs. masking smiles) in photographs report greater well-being and marital satisfaction thirty years later (Harker and Keltner 2001). Another study found that having a Duchenne smile in a yearbook was significantly correlated with longevity (Abel and Kruger 2010).

11. The Self Strikes Out

In contrast to catharsis theory, research has shown that venting anger is not an effective method of defusing it. In one study, participants who ruminated on the person who had angered them and who hit a punching bag were angrier and more aggressive as a result than those who distracted themselves or did nothing at all (Bushman 2002).

Mischkowski and colleagues (2012), in researching anger that results from interpersonal provocation, found self-distancing to be a more effective anger management strategy than "immersing" oneself in the situation. Imagining oneself to be an observer diffuses hostility and prevents the acting out of rage. The study shows how detachment can allow one to behave less aggressively and stay present with distressing situations and emotions.

***

Self-construal can shape the way people understand and express their emotions. One study comparing American and Japanese samples found a relationship between type of self-construal (valuing autonomy and independence vs. valuing connection and interdependence) and anger regulation (Akutsu et al. 2016). Among the Americans, a positive association was found between having independent self-construal and expressing anger outward, and a negative association between independent self-construal and suppressing anger inward. In the Japanese sample, a positive association between anger control and life satisfaction was found.

***

The relationship between anger and autobiographical memory was investigated by Hung and Bryant (2016). They found that participants with higher dispositional anger, when provoked, reported more anger-related autobiographical memories in which they were the agents of the anger. They propose that those individuals who hold the self-perception of being an angry person are more likely to recall memories associated with this perception. When states of anger are ignited by interpersonal provocation, participants tend to recall more memories of themselves as the targets of anger or injustice.

***

In a study of research participants who were insulted and induced to ruminate (Denson et al. 2008), subjective feelings of anger were correlated with activity in the dorsal anterior cingulate cortex, a region associated with distress related to pain and social rejection (Kross et al. 2007). Rumination was correlated with activity in the medial prefrontal cortex, a region associated with self-awareness of emotions and cognition (Macrae et al. 2004; Ochsner et al. 2004). Rumination tended to follow activation in the hippocampus, insula, and cingulate cortex, supporting theories that rumination is a multifaceted emotional response pattern that maintains negative affect.

Imaging studies have shown that, when anger is induced, blood flow increases in the left ventromedial prefrontal cortex, the area responsible for constraining impulsive outbursts. An inverse response, decreased blood flow, is found in the left amygdala, the region responsible for fight or flight activation (Dougherty et al. 2004). Among patients with major depressive disorder, less blood flow was observed, during anger induction, to the left ventrome-dial prefrontal cortex, and greater blood flow to the left amygdala, revealing the possible mechanism for a connection between depression and anger attacks.

12. The Self Steals Credit

Agency, the sense of controlling one's actions, is a key component of the subjective experience of self-consciousness and a way to differentiate oneself from others (Gallagher 2000). Differentiations have been made between the feeling of agency and the judgment of agency. One feels the agent of their actions secondary to *nonconceptual, low-level sensorimotor processes* (feeling in control of our voluntary actions even if not thinking about them). One judges oneself as an agent of action via explicit, conceptual attribution (Synofzik et al. 2008). Studies have demonstrated that our experience of agency does not necessarily match objective reality; i.e., feeling in control does not equate with actually being in control. In other words, the brain can construct a sense of agency (Moore 2016).

The theory of apparent mental causation posits that there are uncon-scious causal pathways that are responsible for our actions, as opposed to our intentions (Wegner 2002). The comparator model, in contrast, proposes that actions start with our goals/intentions that send signals to the motor control systems which generate a response and sensory feedback (Frith et al. 2000). A cue integration model combines aspects of both, arguing that a sense of agency stems from a variety of sources of information (Moore and Fletcher 2012).

Sense of body ownership ("I am the one moving") has been differenti-ated from sense of agency ("I am the one moving my body"). Both have been described as prereflexive parts of experience; i.e., low-level sensory-motor processes that generate a minimal awareness of embodied action (Tsakiris et al. 2007).

***

The brain mechanisms behind one's sense of agency have just recently begun to be studied (Haggard 2017). Activation in the temporo-parietal junction has been associated with sense of agency. More specifically, neuro-imaging studies have found activation in different brain regions when people experience external agency attribution vs. self-agency attribution (Sperduti et al. 2011).

13. The Self Is Selfish

Self-centeredness has been found to vary as a function of one's social class and wealth. Studies reveal that those in a lower socioeconomic class demonstrate greater dispositional compassion and greater activation of compassion in the face of others' suffering than those in an upper class (Stellar et al. 2012), as well as greater empathic accuracy (e.g., the ability to correctly judge the emotions of others) (Kraus et al. 2010).

Other research has found that having less correlates with giving more: lower socioeconomic class participants were found to be more generous, helpful, trusting, and charitable than their upper-class research counterparts (Piff et al. 2010). Simply making people feel more wealthy (regardless of actual income) by having them compare themselves to others worse off was found to lead to more selfish, unethical choices and greedy behavior (Piff et al. 2012).

A series of nine experiments found that priming people to think about money leads to a more self-sufficient orientation in which people are less likely to request help and help others (Vohs et al. 2006). Reminders of money also cause people to want to work and play alone, and physically distance themselves from a new acquaintance to a greater degree than those not prompted to think about money.

***

Results from a series of ten experiments show that people who deliberate longer about how much to contribute give less than those who decide quickly. Selfishness appears to be a function of mulling over the decision, whereas the intuitive gut response tends to be one of more generosity (Rand et al. 2012). Automatic, intuitive processes, as opposed to deliberative decision making, were also found to be associated with occurrences of high-stakes altruism in which individuals risked their lives to save others (Rand and Epstein 2014).

***

Current evolutionary theory and mathematical models explain why generosity and cooperation have evolved in nature (Stewart and Plotkin 2013). Even at the molecular level, there are examples of the cooperative behavior of proteins and genes (not just "selfish genes") in the origin and evolution of life (Penny 2014). Studies of identical and fraternal twins show evidence of genetic effects on sharing behavior and empathy (Robison 2014). Specific genes have been linked to altruistic behavior (Avinun et al. 2011). Research on the prefrontal cortex's role in sharing behavior has demonstrated an innate predisposition toward prosocial (helping and giving) behavior when cognitive control is reduced (Christov-Moore et al. 2017). In other words, the prefrontal cortex may restrain our default selflessness and generosity.

Studies of eighteen- and twenty-four-month-old children show that toddlers peaceably and equally divide items that have not yet been in their possession. These results demonstrate that young children are generous when sorting resources among themselves (Ulber et al. 2015). Verbal socialization has also been found to affect whether children will behave selfishly or generously. One study found that explicitly talking with one's children about giving to charity increased the probability of the children giving by 18.5 percent (Wilhelm et al. 2016). Parents' role modeling of giving did not have an effect.

14. The Self Gets Rejected

In a series of five studies, researchers found that recovery after rejection varies in response to whether one changes their self-definition (Howe and

Dweck 2015). Specifically, people who believe that personality cannot be changed report alterations in their self-definition when reflecting on past rejections (e.g., they question their true or core self), which causes them to experience ongoing negative emotions and fear the recurrence of rejection. Those who believe personality can be changed do not experience disturbance to their self-definition after rejection and recover more quickly.

***

Correlations have been found between low self-esteem and high *rejection sensitivity* (the tendency to anxiously expect rejection) (Berenson and Downey 2006). Rejection sensitivity has been theorized as part of a defensive motivational system that activates and mobilizes to protect the self. The system generates behaviors such as pleasing others, trying to gain acceptance, and prediction of hostile or negative reactions from others. The strategy chosen depends upon how much control one feels one can have on the outcome. People who are low in self-esteem also tend to be low in self-efficacy, making them less likely to engage in rejection-prevention strategies when faced with rejection cues (Sommer and Baumeister 2002).

***

Neural responses to social rejection have been studied, identifying through fMRI that the rostral anterior cingulate cortex, a brain region associated with emotional control, is involved in attenuating negative reactions to social rejection (Gyurak et al. 2012). People with low self-esteem were found to evaluate social rejection as less arousing and less rejecting when they demonstrated high *attentional control*, the ability to direct and maintain attentional focus. The strongest physiological reactivity to social stress was found in the sample with low self-esteem and low attentional control.

***

Research shows that people tend to overestimate the impact of rejection and interpersonal setbacks, underestimating the many coping skills they have for recovering from them (Wilson and Gilbert 2003). People cope and repair themselves, for example, by derogating those that reject them or by assuming that the rejectors didn't really know them to begin with (Bourgeois and Leary 2001).

***

In a series of studies, social rejection was found to have a positive effect in enhancing creativity, but only among those participants who demonstrated an independent self-concept (Kim et al. 2013). In general, those motivated to think of themselves as separate from others or to value their individuality, tend to be less sensitive to rejection and less in need of fitting in. Those with independent self-construal and a need for uniqueness were found to be more creative following rejection than those with an interdependent self-concept.

15. The Self Checks Out

Emotional numbing has been found to be a symptom of trauma and post-traumatic stress disorder (e.g., Kashdan et al. 2006). Among combat veterans, greater emotional numbing has also been linked to major depression. Detachment and expressive inhibition have been explored as responses to stress, with corresponding physiological markers: attenuated sympathetic and parasympathetic recovery to stress exposure (Clapp et al. 2015).

***

Research has begun to identify molecular and cellular changes associated with stress and vulnerability to addiction (Sinha 2008). Stress that is chronic, uncontrollable, unpredictable (as opposed to "good" stress that is moderate, time limited, and associated with mastery and excitement) functions as a risk factor for addiction. Increasing levels of emotional distress have been linked to increases in impulsivity, decreases in control, and more maladaptive behaviors. Neurobiological correlates to this include a decrease in prefrontal functioning and increased limbic-striatal responding (Li and Sinha 2008). In animal studies, exposure to stress results in increased seeking and self-administration of opiods, alcohol, and psychostimulants (Cleck and Blendy 2008; Lu et al. 2003).

Specific stressors related to increased vulnerability to addiction include early adverse life events, trauma, and child maltreatment. Early life stress affects development of the prefrontal cortex, which is integral in the activation and regulation of autonomic responses to stress (Gratton and Sullivan 2005).

***

Studies on compulsive buying demonstrate that it is used as a means of elevating one's mood, and that it contains the same behavioral elements as other addictions (Clark and Calleja 2008). A consistent relationship has been found between compulsive buying and low self-esteem, impulsiveness, and loneliness (Faber and O'Guinn 1992).

16. The Self Stays Stuck

According to self-concept theory, people tend to ascribe to a *self-consistency standard* (the belief that the self should be stable and consistent) and a *self-enhancement standard* (the belief that one should be able to improve oneself). When these standards are violated, such as in the face of a perceived failure, the violation is associated with both a decrease in positive mental health and an increase in negative mental health (Keyes 2000).

Similarly, researchers have found a relationship between an emotional state of threat (e.g., insecurity and fear of failure) and cognitive rigidity (Pally 1955). Cognitive rigidity has also been associated with poorer memory recall (Cosden et al. 1979), greater intolerance toward ambiguity, and authoritarianism (Duncan and Peterson 2014). Psychological inflexibility has been identified as a negative predictor of psychological health (Woodruff et al. 2014).

***

Cultural differences have been found in how rigidly people hold on to their self-concepts. East Asians demonstrate greater change, spontaneity, and inconsistency in their self-beliefs when compared to Euro-Americans who demonstrate less tolerance for contradiction and holism in such self-knowledge (Spencer-Rogers et al. 2009).

***

Change has been found to cause stress. In the workplace, for instance, organizational changes cause stress especially when they have consequences for employees' self-construal, or sense of self (Wisse and Sleebos 2016). When people allow their meaning making to accommodate to the change and stressful experiences in their lives, they are more likely to experience a positive modification of self-concept and post-traumatic growth (Horita 2013). In response to threatening health communications, self-affirmations have been found to lead to behavior change via neural self-related processing (Falk et al. 2015).

***

The sensory and emotional imprint of trauma, which takes shape separately from the semantic representation of trauma in memory, has been well-documented in the neuroimaging and neurobiological literature (e.g., Van der Kolk 2000). Establishment of safety and control, anxiety management, and emotional processing (rather than traditional verbal reliving/meaning making of traumatic events) are key components of effective trauma treatment.

Animal studies have shown that reliving fear-memories (or having trouble extinguishing fear-memories) differentiates those who develop post-traumatic symptoms following traumatic events from those who don't (Park and Chung 2016). Animal studies also show that when early stressors are overcome and lead to the enhancing of emotion processing, cognitive control, and neuroendocrine regulation, they can lead to resilience and stress inoculation rather than stress-related mental and physical impairment (Lyons and Parker 2007).

17. The Self Second-Guesses

Judgmental self-doubt has been studied by scientists and found to be associated with procrastination, anxiety, depression, discomfort with uncertainty, and a greater need for approval from others (Mirels et al. 2002). No differences were found between high and low self-doubters on measures of intelligence, but high self-doubters give less weight to their own interpretations and views, making them more susceptible to psychological distress.

Intellectual self-doubt (doubt concerning one's intellectual abilities) has been found in other studies to be distinct from intellect (Hardy et al. 2010). Grade point average and standardized test scores did not correlate with self-doubt.

***

Self-doubt and self-esteem have been found to be correlated, with those higher in self-doubt experiencing lower self-esteem (Oleson et al. 2000), although this finding may only pertain to those who tend to evaluate their self-worth based on judgments of performance competence (Wichman and Hermann 2010).

Studies have investigated how self-doubt impacts not only performance competence, but also relationships. For those with low self-esteem, self-doubt has been found to lead to behaviors of distancing oneself from one's partner and also questioning the partner's positive regard for them as well as the standing of the relationship in general (Murray et al. 1998). Other research has found correlations between self-doubt and low relationship satisfaction, underestimation of one's partner's love, and fewer positive feelings about one's partner (Murray et al. 2001).

***

Strategies for coping with self-doubt include self-handicapping, over-achieving, and *other-enhancement* (believing one's competitor benefits from certain advantages) (Braslow et al. 2012). Researchers emphasize that different components of self-doubt, such as deficits in self-competence vs. deficits in self-liking, result in the need for different coping strategies, though all components pertain to an underlying uncertainty about the self.

18. The Self Suffers Scarcity

Researchers have found that a scarcity mindset impacts cognitive capacity, making people prone to poorer decision making (Novotney 2014). Scarcity depletes cognitive bandwidth, causing people to focus on urgent here-and-now concerns at the expense of planning for the future or resisting temptations in the moment (Heshmat 2015). A scarcity mindset is also correlated with preoccupation with trade-off decision making, deciding between urgent needs vs. what's important, leading to decision fatigue. Depletion leaves one more susceptible to impulses and unable to make minor choices (Baumeister and Tierney 2012).

Scarcity thoughts create a distraction disrupting higher-level thinking. Simply being preoccupied with financial concerns makes people engage less of their IQ than those not facing such concerns. When attention is tunneled into worries about having enough money, cognitive abilities, or *fluid intelligence*, is lost elsewhere (Mani et al. 2013). Scarcity regarding time has been found to have the same effect, with busy people who are preoccupied with not having enough time more likely to fail to manage their time efficiently (Mullainathan and Shafir 2013).

***

Scarcity thinking can lead to a planning fallacy in which one assumes the future will hold more time, money, etc. than the present. This predisposes one toward borrowing from the future (Zauberman and Lynch 2005). Studies have shown that those who dwell on resource scarcity are more likely to spend money on self-improvement, especially among those who most desire control (Roux et al. 2015). Thinking about scarcity can also lead to generous behavior, but only if such behavior confers an indirect benefit to oneself.

***

One study explored the positive effects of having participants imagine that time was scarce such that they only had one month to live in the city where they were located. These participants demonstrated greater life satisfaction and positive emotions than the control group (Layous et al. 2017). Temporal scarcity in this study appeared to activate more savoring of the present moment, linked to greater well-being.

19. The Self Erodes

Demo (1992) reviews research data suggesting that self-concept reflects a "baseline view" of oneself over time, even though self-evaluation can be situationally variable. He defines self-concept as a structure as well as a process; i.e., a dynamic structure that responds and revises itself with new situational stimuli.

***

Identity theory proposes that roles develop into role-identities. Self-structure is affected by role-identities to the extent to which (1) they involve subjectively important social interactions and relationships (Merolla et al. 2012), and (2) the extent to which they are salient; e.g., how likely it is that a particular role-identity will be active across situations (Morris 2013).

Thoits (1991) combines identity theory with stress research, positing that differences in how people experience psychological distress due to social status disparity may be explained in part by whether or not identity-threatening stressors are present. Difficulties that impact a domain of identity may be perceived as more challenging and less workable than difficulties affecting other life domains. De-emphasizing the importance of a particular role (by not having it be a source of identity or self-evaluation) in the face of role-related stressors has been suggested as a strategy for coping with social-role-related adversity (Thoits 2012).

The role enhancement or identity accumulation hypothesis proposes that the more roles one holds, the greater one's well-being. Research has confirmed the relationship between multiple-role involvement and mental health, as defined by increased autonomy, environmental mastery, personal growth, positive relations with others, purpose in life, and self-acceptance (Ahrens et al. 2006).

***

Self-affirmation theory addresses how people cope with threats to the self and maintain a sense of being moral, efficacious, "good enough." In their literature review, Cohen and Sherman (2014) found that when people face challenges to their self's integrity, *self-affirmations* (acts that demonstrate one's adequacy) can expand their view of the self and its resources and remind one of their core values. In the face of challenges and life changes, self-affirmations remind one of what really matters. Self-affirmation interventions have been applied to the fields of education, health, and interpersonal and group relations.

When threats are encountered by a self that has been "affirmed" or a self that is in touch with its most expansive view of itself, they have less negative impact on psychological well-being (Sherman et al. 2013). When affirmed, the self is also less likely to engage in short-term defensive responses such as denial, rumination, spin control, putting down others, and other protective strategies (Sherman and Cohen 2006).

20. The Self Dies

Death anxiety has been found to display a bimodal distribution, spiking in men and women in their twenties and again, among women only, in their fifties (Russac 2007). Higher levels of death anxiety have been correlated with lower ego integrity and more psychological difficulties in elderly adults (Fortner and Neimeyer 1999).

***

Terror management theory proposes that people experience a conscious terror of death, given an instinctual drive toward survival and inevitable mortality (Greenberg et al. 1997). The fear of annihilation of body, mind, and soul leads individuals and cultures to suppress the fear of death by developing ways to achieve symbolic immortality. Self-esteem has been hypothesized to act as a buffer or defense mechanism in the face of annihilation fears, albeit outside conscious awareness (Cicirelli 2002). Researchers have found that reminders of one's mortality do increase self-esteem striving, and that high levels of self-esteem reduce accessibility of death-related thoughts (Pyszczynski et al. 2004).

High levels of creative goals and achievement were found in one study to be associated with lower death-thought accessibility among participants exposed to mortality salience. Creativity may play a role in creating symbolic immortality and thus produce an existential anxiety buffer (Perach and Wisman 2016).

***

One study showed that less mindful individuals, when faced with mortality salience, demonstrated greater self-esteem striving than those high in mindfulness (Niemiec et al. 2010). Mindful individuals were found to engage in less suppression of death thoughts when confronted with mortality salience. Thus, those more receptive to their present experience, as opposed to those engaged in private self-reflection, may be better equipped to think of mortality when prompted and be less subject to death-related terror.

21. No-Self: The Biggest Bang

A factor analysis of common underlying dimensions of spirituality across China, India, and the United States revealed unifying interconnectedness or oneness with all other beings to be a key factor (McClintock et al. 2016). Love as a sacred reality was also identified as a common factor. Both of these factors were associated with less risk for psychopathology across all countries.

The construct of self-transcendence has been operationalized and validated in studies (Levenson et al. 2005). In people under twenty-nine years of age, ego transcendence was found to predict general psychological resilience, whereas for those older than twenty-nine, spiritual transcendence (oneness and timelessness) was associated with resilience (Hanfstingl 2013). Spiritual oneness beliefs, more strongly related to spirituality than to traditional religiousness, have been found to be negatively associated with depression, anxiety, and negative affect, and positively associated with proenvironmental attitudes and behavior (Garfield et al. 2014).

***

New models of consciousness elucidate the apparent dualism of a materially based mind and a universal quantum consciousness. Within the field of biophysics, a proposal has been made for further investigation of the nature of the self as a unified self-awareness with a central creative role in organizing processes of the physical world (Kauffman 2015).

A new model of self has also been proposed in theoretical immunology in which self is viewed as less static and persistent than the traditional enlightenment construct of the self. This "incorporative" model, borrowed from non-Western contexts, views what is other-than-the-body as an opportunity for "creative assimilation of difference," rather than viewing it as an enemy to protect and defend against (Napier 2012).

Unity of consciousness theories have addressed "the law of coherence" across systems, the cooperative way energy-information is communicated among all parts within and across organisms, contributing to an evolving planetary consciousness (Montecucco 2006). Montecucco (2016) discusses the "consciousness (r)evolution paradigm," a holistic model that accounts for mind-body unity within individuals and among peoples as well as for a global unitary evolutionary process. The dissociation between individuals as a result of conventional ego-centered reality has been identified as a current challenge for continued conscious systems development at the planetary level (Germine 1997).

***

A neurocognitive frame for the "resting mind" has been proposed that draws upon the neurophenomenology of nonconceptual or nondual awareness (Vago and Zeidan 2016). In addition, neural correlates of nondual awareness during meditation have been studied (Josipovic 2013). Neuroscientists have identified regions of the brain that activate during transcendental self-awareness, specifically the left and right parietal systems (Urgesi et al. 2010). The self-transcendence trait has also been found to be associated with the serotonin transporter availability in the brainstem (Kim et al. 2015). Self-transcending meditation has been found to have a different EEG band (characterized by alpha 1 activity) than meditations based upon either focused attention or open monitoring (Travis and Shear 2010).

Neural substrates of unified compassionate awareness have been mapped using EEG data collected on advanced meditators (Schoenberg et al. 2017). During nondual, compassionate meditative states, current density decreases occur in regions regulating self-reference and executive control.

In a meta-analysis of fMRI studies, different patterns of neural activation were found in Buddhist mindfulness meditation as compared to Hindu-inspired meditation focused on loss of sense of self and duality (Tomasino et al. 2014). Frontal lobe activation was associated with the mindfulness approach, whereas activation in a left-lateralized network of areas was associated with the nondual meditation.

22. No-Self: Fuel Efficient

A seminal study by Lisbet et al. (1983) found that movement in the body, as measured by first brain potential, begins many milliseconds before conscious awareness about the voluntary movement takes place. The researchers concluded that unconscious neural processes make the decisions about movement, raising questions about freedom of choice.

These results and their replication have been recently challenged based on concerns about the methods used for assessing consciousness (Guggisberg and Mottaz 2013). Use of other methods reveals that conscious intention may not appear instantaneously but builds up gradually, reflecting, in these experiments, decisions that are indeed conscious but not yet finalized, still allowing for the possibility of free will.

***

Relaxed spontaneity (i.e., "not trying") was recognized as linked to personal and social success by early Chinese thinkers. This idea is regaining popularity in modern psychology. The powerful role that embodied, tacit knowledge plays in human behavior tends to support this ideal of effortless action (Slingerland 2014). Slingerland (2015) discusses the science behind spontaneous action, drawing parallels with the Chinese wu wei (effortless action) school of philosophy. He presents examples of athletes and actors who demonstrate an alternative to overactive cognitive-emotional control. He also reviews the imaging experiments that show a deactivation in their lateral prefrontal cortexes (which induces deliberate, controlled problem solving).

A study of middle and high school students' experiences with both effortful and effortless attention found that effortless attention helps students focus better on tasks without much effort (Csikszentmihalyi 2010). Studies investigating the psychology of perception have found that, with difficult visual tasks, active trying can be less effective than a relaxed stance of letting answers "pop out" (Smilek et al. 2006; Watson et al. 2010). Research on motor learning has found that greater focus on the effects of movement enhances movement efficiency compared to focus on the movement itself. This finding of so-called "effortless movement" has been replicated in a range of studies on sports performance (Wulf 2010).

***

Neuroscience has begun to identify how the brain responds when people observe the pain of others. An individual, for example, will experience distinct neural reactivity in the face of another's suffering, demonstrating a level of interpersonal interconnectivity. The interconnectivity is not limited to humans, as the same activation in the same neural regions (dorsal anterior cingulate cortex, bilateral anterior insula) occurs when one witnesses pain and harm inflicted upon other biological entities, specifically animals and nature. Humans are not alone in responding in this way (Mathur et al. 2016).

The neurobiology of altruism has been linked to the social-motivational design of the brain and the presence of the hormone peptide oxytocin (Hurlemann and Marsh 2016). Neuroscientists propose that a combination of social motivation and empathy, called *the camaraderie effect*, prompts altruistic helping behavior in animals, which also contributes to their own physiological well-being (Lahvis 2017). Experiments have confirmed the empathy-altruism model that empathy fuels altruistic motivation, separate from the motivation associated with egalitarianism or selflessness (Van Lange 2008). Researchers have found that empathy leads to a greater sense of self-other overlap or oneness (Cialdini et al. 1997). In this sense, helping others does not necessarily stem from altruism or selflessness, but from empathic concern's signaling of oneness.

An fMRI study links empathic and prosocial responses to the generation and enhancement of other-related mental representations. These representations have been found to override one's own perspective rather than being sourced from projections of one's own mental state (Majdandzic et al. 2016).

***

Generative concern has been associated with life satisfaction (McAdams et al. 1993). A study of mortality among Medicare patients revealed that altruism, generosity, and tender-mindedness were related to increases in median survival time (Costa Jr et al. 2014). Perceptions of one's generativity, as well as actual generative contributions, were associated with decreased odds of activity-of-daily-living disability in older adults, as well as lower odds of dying (Gruenewald et al. 2012).

Other-oriented volunteering has been found to have better health outcomes for people than self-oriented volunteering, though both forms are significantly related to better cumulative health outcomes in general (Yeung et al. 2017). Care-giving behavior has been found to be linked to decreased mortality risk for the caregivers (Brown et al. 2009).

***

Calls have been made for a comparative analysis of the evolution of helping behaviors across human and nonhuman species (Bshary and Raihani 2017). For example, altruistic self-removal behavior has been found among social insect colonies in which infected insect workers remove themselves to prevent disease spread in the colony (Rueppell et al. 2010). The mechanisms underlying cooperative behavior have been explored at the genetic and molecular level, as well as at the level of nongenetic inheritance: parental effects, transgenerational epigenetic effects, ecological and cultural inheritance (Kapser et al. 2017).

23. No-Self: The Better Lover

Sociocognitive neuroscience has found that the mirror neuron system (in which one's mirror neurons activate when watching another person take action) may be involved in love relationships, facilitating an individual's understanding of their beloved's intentions (Ortigue and Bianchi-Demicheli 2008).

***

Research on love and the brain have found that, in addition to activating neural reward systems, the feeling of love also deactivates the neural pathways for such emotions as fear and social judgment (Song et al. 2015). Studies using fMRI have shown love-related alterations in the workings of the brain such as an increase in the functional connectivity within the reward, motivation, emotion regulation, and social cognition networks. Similar reward and attentional network activation was found among Mormon practitioners experiencing spiritual feelings during their devotional practice (Ferguson et al. 2016).

Love has been described as a stress-reducing, health-promoting neurobiological phenomenon involving limbic processes and oxytocin, endorphins, dopamine, and other mechanisms (Esch and Stefano 2005a). The central nervous system's activity pattern associated with love may have protective effects on the brain (Esch and Stefano 2005b). MRI studies identifying the neural underpinnings of unconditional love find that it is associated with a specific neural network distinct from that of other emotions (Beauregard et al. 2009). This network includes structures involved in the brain's reward systems and cerebral structures involved in romantic and maternal love.

A longitudinal study of married couples showed that degree of spiritual intimacy (as reported by both spouses) predicted more positivity and less negativity in marital behavior (Kusner et al. 2014). Particular spiritual cognitions have been found to foster marital satisfaction of older couples, especially compassionate love and sanctification of marriage (Sabey et al. 2014).

***

Studies show that mindfulness reduces performance- and body-related insecurities and distractions during sexual activity for men and women. It has also been found to enhance sexual satisfaction (Dunkley et al. 2015). Increases in nonjudgmental present-moment awareness, after a group mindfulness-based therapy, were found to predict improvement in sexual desire in women (Brotto and Basson 2014). The *creative self-forgetfulness* component of self-transcendence, defined as a proneness to mind-altering attentional absorption, has also been found to predict female desire and arousal (Costa et al. 2016).

24. No-Self, No Shoulding

A study of contributory factors to road rage identified attribution of blame to others, high life stress, and displaced anger among other psychological causes of hostile driving behavior (Sansone and Sansone 2010). Another study found that illusion-of-control beliefs predict aggressive driving (Stephens and Ohtsuka 2014).

Moral anger (anger linked to the welfare of others or the greater good of society as a whole) has been explored in terms of its prosocial role in improving organizational practices (Lindebaum and Geddes 2015). The authors differentiate moral anger from personal anger with moral outrage, righteous anger, indignation, and empathic anger in terms of moral anger being other-focused and prompting corrective behaviors without intent to harm. Moral anger is also a primary appraisal; i.e., its sympathetic arousal is directly triggered by unjust external situations and an automatic, unconscious knowing of something being wrong (vs. a more deliberative appraisal of personal affront).

In a study of the most effective motives for sustaining environmental activists, self-determination theory's intrinsic motivation (motivation stemming from the satisfaction of behavior for its own sake) was found to be the best predictor of nonburnout. Activist commitment was associated with *integrated motivation* (motivation fueled by a desire for certain extrinsic goals but sourced from a desire to be an autonomous, integrity-based agent of one's life) (Sheldon et al. 2016).

***

Adults have been found to display a *negativity bias*, a tendency to focus on and use negative information more often than positive information in making sense of the world (Vaish et al. 2008). This bias affects judgment and decision making as well as the impressions formed of others and attributions made about their traits. Neuroscience has also found evidence of a negativity bias in that negative stimuli receive greater neural processing than positive stimuli. In infants as early as seven months of age, trends toward bias have been found in terms of increased attention toward negative emotional expression, suggesting an evolutionary benefit of the negativity bias in helping avoid potential harmful stimuli.

Research on the acceptance of negative emotions (vs. avoidance or displacement of those feelings) has found that acceptance protects individuals from negative affect during the negative emotion situation and also protects them from developing depression symptoms after stressful life experiences (Shallcross et al. 2010).

25. No-Self, No Calories

In a meta-analysis of studies on rigidity of thought and behavior, researchers (Shultz and Searleman 2002) found that rigidity is negatively related to intelligence and positively related to authoritarianism, especially in stressful situations. A curvilinear relationship was found between age and *attitudinal rigidity* (the tendency to create and perseverate on certain mental and behavioral sets) with rigidity decreasing modestly with age until it increases after early old age. Low levels of rigidity have been found to be predicted by the presence of stimulating environmental conditions such as complex work environments (Schooler et al. 1999).

Psychological flexibility, defined in part by the ability to shift mindsets and behavioral repertoires, has recently been explored as a fundamental component of health and well-being (Kashdan 2010). Psychological flexibility, a dynamic capacity to adapt to fluctuating situational demands, allows an individual to change perspective and reconfigure mental resources, enabling maintenance of balance and adherence to core values. The benefits of such flexibility include greater adjustment following stressful life events, increased self-determination (vs. extrinsically motivated actions), improved job performance and satisfaction, increased daily activity among pain patients, and health benefits often attributed to those with ego resilience.

A connection has been found between psychological inflexibility and psychopathology (Kashdan 2010). Inflexible rumination and attributional styles, for example, are markers of depression. The behavioral inflexibility of avoidance predisposes and exacerbates anxiety. Psychological inflexibility with prejudiced thoughts has been found to predict generalized prejudice (Levin et al. 2016). Personality dimensions such as neuroticism may complicate efforts toward psychological flexibility, whereas dimensions such as positive affect, conscientiousness, and openness to experience may enhance it (Kashdan 2010).

***

Mindfulness practice has been found to reduce cognitive rigidity, allowing practitioners to not be "blinded" by past experience. Experienced meditators may thus be more likely to engage new and adaptive ways of responding to situations (Greenberg et al. 2012). Vipassana meditation in particular correlated in one study with a change in ego defense mechanisms, allowing for greater tolerance of common stressors, less impulsiveness, and greater maturity (Emavardhana and Tori 1997).

Mindfulness has been found to be negatively associated with neuroticism (which is positively associated with psychological inflexibility) (Latzman and Masuda 2013). In one study, psychological flexibility and mindfulness were both found to be negatively associated with somatization, depression, anxiety, and general psychological distress among a nonclinical sample of college students (Masuda and Tully 2011).

26. No-Self, No-Judgment

Social judgment theory proposes that attitudes change as a result of evaluating ideas in comparison to current attitudes supported by a person's environment or social context (Sherif and Hovland 1980). Attitudes are thus acquired and influenced by what individuals deem as (un)acceptable to others, especially to members of their group.

Research on judgmental biases has found that one's emotions and motivations also strongly influence reasoning processes (for instance, happy participants form more positive impressions of others and make more favorable judgments than when sad) (Forgas and Bower 1987). In addition, nonconscious processes such as tapping into cultural stereotypes or automatically categorizing stimuli as "good" or "bad" (Schwarz 2000) influence opinions and decision making. Social psychologists argue that attitudes might, thus, be better understood as processes of evaluative judgment rather than as stable, enduring constructs.

***

Studies have identified core dimensions of social judgment: morality, sociability, and competence (Fiske et al. 2007; Brambilla and Leach 2014). Evaluating the sociability or "warmth" of another helps to determine whether or not that person is likely to be a friend or foe, and evaluation of competence offers information about how likely it is that the other will enact their good or bad intentions. Perceiving others as warm and competent has been found to produce (in the one perceiving) positive emotions and to elicit positive behaviors (such as admiration and helping behavior); whereas, negativity (for instance, contempt) is elicited when perceiving others as cold and incompetent. When people are judged as high on one dimension and low on another, ambivalent affect and behavior get directed toward them (e.g., pity, benign neglect, envy). Researchers have found a *compensation bias* in which those perceived as competent are more likely to also be perceived as colder (less sociable). Those perceived as incompetent tend to also be perceived as warmer (more sociable) (Kervyn et al. 2013).

Morality, as defined by honesty and trustworthiness, has been found to play a primary role in how individuals evaluate other individuals as well as groups. Judgments about group-level morality have been found to be more influential in the positive feelings associated with group self-concept than judgments about group competence or sociability (Leach et al. 2007). Researchers have found that those who engage in moral judgment about absolute "wrong" behavior are perceived by others as more moral and trustworthy and are more likely to be chosen as social partners (Everett et al. 2016). The scientists conclude a possible evolutionary advantage to the overt demonstration of moral judgment and the preconscious evaluative process of others' morality.

***

Neuroscientists have found that the brain can make judgments about a face's trustworthiness even before the image of the face is consciously perceived. Parts of the amygdala have been identified as responsible for such evaluation of social cues in the absence of awareness (Freeman et al. 2014).

27. No-Self, No Time to Lose

Ongoing research efforts explore the subjective sense of time, trying to identify an "internal clock" (Allman et al. 2014). Cognitive science has found that the perception of time tends to be rooted in interoceptive states of the body and emotional states of the mental self.

Changes in time perception have been found to occur during childhood, developing along with maturing neural structures (Droit-Volet 2013). Studies have shown that temporal perception is also affected by how many events, or event markers, take place during a time interval (Zauberman et al. 2009). If few events come to mind, the perception of time tends to not persist. The more intervening events remembered in a time interval, the longer the interval seems. In other words, the passage of time is memory dependent.

A decreased awareness of the self is associated with diminished awareness of time (Whittmann 2015a). Other factors that affect the perception of time include routine (Avni-Babad and Ritov 2003). Researchers found that when time is spent in a routine activity, the duration of that time is remembered as being shorter as compared to reports of duration for nonroutine activities. *Cognitive load*—i.e., the demands on attention and working memory—has also been found to affect perception of time duration (Block et al. 2010).

Engagement in narrative, as measured by watching narrative videos, was found to result in a more uniform perception of time in which actual duration of neural processing of the stimuli was in sync with time perception (Cohen et al. 2017). This finding may underlie the experience of time proceeding faster when attention is captured.

A negative perspective on the past has been found to be associated with a subjective sense of time pressure and time expansion, whereas emphasis on a future perspective is associated with a perception of a faster passage of time (Whittman et al. 2015b). Those who demonstrate increased emotion regulation also report a slower passage of the past ten years. Hedonism in the present was found to be associated with a perception of a faster passage of the last week.

***

A study of mindfulness meditators found that they experience less time pressure and a perception of slower passage of time compared to controls (Whittman et al. 2015a). No differences were found between the meditators and control group in how they performed on psychophysical tasks measuring accuracy of time perception. Mindfulness meditation exercises have been found to increase sensitivity to time and increase perception of time dilation (Droit-Volet et al. 2015). Decreased anxiety among experienced meditators was also found to be associated with increased time sensitivity.

28. No-Self, No Tests

Trust has been explored by social scientists as a relational phenomenon (Frederiksen 2014). Trust researchers have identified dimensions of interpersonal trust—ability, benevolence, and integrity—and have investigated how positive and negative emotions mediate the breaches that result from violations of these trustworthiness expectations (Chen et al. 2011). The strategic nature of trust has been debated, with trust exchanges viewed as complex reciprocities including the masking of calculativeness (Reich-Graefe 2014).

Interpersonal trust has been investigated cross-culturally, with the findings that younger people, people with poor self-rated health, and people with lower income demonstrate lower trust (Ward et al. 2014). Trust in family and neighbors was found to be consistently high, whereas variation was found across countries for trust in strangers, foreigners, and people with different religions.

A study on interpersonal trust and self-rated health in China found that out-group and in-group trust was associated with good health (Feng et al. 2016). However, at the province level, high social trust in people in general was found to be negatively associated with good health. A study of forty US communities found different effects of individual perceptions of social trust (Subramanian et al. 2002). People who demonstrate high trust experience the health-promoting effects of community social trust. For those with low trust, the opposite effect was found: poorer health associated with community social trust.

***

Neuroscientists have investigated how the neuropeptide oxytocin can facilitate social interactions, especially after trust has been broken (Baumgartner et al. 2008). Oxytocin may decrease fear mechanisms (reducing activation in the amygdala and midbrain regions) involved in avoidance, allowing for increased social risk taking.

***

A positive relationship has been found between workplace spirituality and trust, with trust mediating the impact of workplace spirituality on job satisfaction (Hassan et al. 2016). The relationship between religion and trust was examined using an experimental trust game (Tan and Vogel 2008). Results showed that participants trusted those who were more religious. This effect was more pronounced among those who were religious themselves.

An epidemiological study, however, found no relationship between religiosity and level of trust in others (Welch et al. 2007). Older members of denominations were found, though, to be more trusting of strangers. A study of twenty-five years of social survey data found that, among certain congregations, trust in others is bolstered by attendance (liberal Protestants), whereas trust is dependent upon affiliation for other congregations (conservative denominations) (Daniels and von der Ruhr 2010).

29. No-Self: Selfless Parenting

Longitudinal studies show that origins of parenting stress can be found in parents' individual and marital satisfaction prior to becoming parents (Kline et al. 1991). Lower self-esteem and job satisfaction prior to parenthood, for example, predicts stress in the parent-child relationship at eighteen months. Other longitudinal studies show that early parenting practices, such as "harsh-conflicted" parenting, have been linked to youth self-regulation issues and alcohol use in early adolescence (Brody and Ge 2001).

Mothers' hostile attribution tendencies have been found to predict children's later externalizing behavior in school (Nix et al. 1999). Maternal childhood trauma was also found to predict offspring internalizing and externalizing difficulties, especially when mothers additionally experienced pre- or postnatal depression (Plant et al. 2017).

Level of maternal ego development was found in one study to be related to level of maternal sensitivity during interaction with infants (Fineman et al. 1997). Mothers at an impulsive level of ego development were found to be less sensitive than mothers at a greater stage of self-awareness, as defined by Loevinger's theory of ego development (Loevinger 1976).

A meta-analysis of studies on parenting and childhood depression found that parental rejection and hostility, but not control, was associated with childhood depression (McLeod et al. 2007a). A meta-analysis of parenting and childhood anxiety revealed the opposite, an association between parental control and anxiety (McLeod et al. 2007b). A review of studies on the relationship between parenting practices and the internalizing behaviors of children identified poor parenting risk factors including overinvolved parenting, permissive parenting, and overreactive parenting, as well as authoritarian parenting (Rose et al. 2017). In several studies, a negative relationship was found between authoritative parenting and internalization symptoms.

***

Parents' conditional regard toward their children (as perceived by their college-age offspring) in the domains of emotion control, academics, sports, and prosocial behavior was found to be related to behavioral enactments, fluctuations in self-esteem, perceived parental disapproval, and resentment of parents (Assor et al. 2004).

A study of the intergenerational transmission of perfectionism found a direct relationship between mothers and daughters' maladaptive perfectionism (Soenens et al. 2005). Parent psychological controlling was found to be the intervening variable in the relationship between parent and child perfectionism.

***

A study investigating parental identity in middle age found that, among men in particular who score higher in parental stress, greater achievement of parental identity was associated with greater psychological and social well-being (Fadjukoff et al. 2016). Parental identity development was also related to greater generativity in both men and women. Authoritative parenting, reflecting a high degree of knowledge about the child's activities and high nurturance, was associated with parental identity achievement.

***

Mindful parenting, involving nonjudgmental, moment-to-moment awareness of the parent-child interaction, is gathering an evidence base as an effective parenting strategy (Duncan et al. 2009). Mindful parenting has been found to facilitate emotional self-regulation in parents and acceptance toward their children, and has been incorporated into family prevention programs, such as the Strengthening Families Program (SFP), an empirically validated family preventive intervention.

A study of children at three different developmental stages found that those who had parents high on dispositional mindfulness (who engaged in more mindful parenting practices and less negative practices) were found to have less internalizing and externalizing behaviors and psychopathology (Parent et al. 2016).

30. No-Self Tastes Better

A literature review of sixty-eight publications on mindful eating reveals that mindful eating practices have been effective in addressing emotional and binge eating (Warren et al. 2017). Increased awareness of internal cues has been found as the mechanism of action, preventing overeating and possibly weight gain, though less evidence exists supporting mindful eating as a weight management strategy. Mindfulness has been theorized as enhancing a somatic focus that reduces competing attention toward internally focused rumination (Kerr et al. 2013).

Intuitive eating (including unconditional permission to eat, reliance on hunger/satiety cues) has been found to be affected by both mindfulness practices and psychological flexibility (Sairanen et al. 2015). Awareness, observation, nonjudgment, nonreactivity, and general psychological flexibility are related but not overlapping constructs linked to regulation of eating practices. Sensory-based eating has been found to correlate with mindful eating and improvement in eating-related attitudes among those concerned with diet and weight control (Gravel et al. 2014).

A study of meal satisfaction in the workplace found that mindful eating contributed to perceived food quality as well as positive associations of perceived ambience at the workplace canteen (Hauggard et al. 2016). A brief mindfulness instruction in one study was found to enhance sensory enjoyment of both pleasurable (chocolate) and neutral (raisin) foods, as well as to lead to lower calorie consumption of unhealthy food (Arch et al. 2016).

***

The neurocognitive bases of food perception have been explored, with a neural homeostatic interoceptive system posited as responsible for integrated awareness of oral and olfactory sensory information (Verhagen 2007). Mindful attention to internal somatic sensations has been found to increase somatosensory sensitivity and to reduce tactile misperception (Mirams et al. 2013).

Participants in one study who were high in "private self-consciousness" (i.e., able to direct their attention) were found to be more accurate in reporting their internal state with regard to the perception of taste than those less able to perform self-directed attention (Scheier et al. 1979). They were also less susceptible to having manipulation of flavor expectations affect their taste perceptions.

31. No-Self, No Lost or Found

Hood (2002) discusses the "lost and found" of the self, its tendency to disappear in mystical experience. He notes that the "transcendent I" or soulful self of mysticism does not necessarily conform to the empirical unity of selfhood as conceived in the psychological literature.

Fingelkurts (2009) reviews the neuroscientific-theological debate regarding whether the brain is hardwired to produce or to perceive God. He presents an integral view of consciousness/spirit and brain/matter in which neither can be reduced to the other, and in which neuroscience and cognitive processes contribute to the description of religious experience.

Rogers and Friedberg (2016) present a model of core consciousness as an inherent property of biological life. Atwood and Maltin (1991) review the multidisciplinary nature of notions of interconnectedness. Parallels are drawn between Eastern mysticism and system theories in psychology, among other trends, with a call for integrating an understanding of global consciousness into Western modes of psychotherapy.

Prabhu and Bhat (2013) provide a comparative analysis of the Cartesian dualism of mind and matter and Eastern Vedantic unity approaches to consciousness. The Vedantic view posits life as essentially cognitive and conscious, a subjective evolution of consciousness rather than an objective evolution of bodies (Shanta 2015). Awakening (into no-self) has been described as an art form, rather than as an achievement or a gathering of knowledge. Letting go of doing allows for direct knowing and experiencing simultaneously (Curtis 2016).

***

Hameroff (2001) proposes a model in which the very structure of brain neurons allows for a manifestation of conscious experience consistent with features of quantum space-time physics. Walton (2017) calls for the development of scientific methods to better explore this relationship between consciousness, spirituality, and recent advances in quantum physics.

32. No-Self, No Lack

Sense of abundance has been explored as a fundamental component of gratitude. Gratitude, in turn, has been associated with subjective well-being

(Watkins et al. 2003). In a study of 136 countries, a relationship was found between the giving away of resources and happiness, even among those countries considered poor (Aknin et al. 2013). Generosity and sharing behavior have also been found to have emotional benefits for young children under two years of age (Aknin et al. 2012).

Researchers have also investigated subjective sense of time affluence, and have found that those who choose to spend time on others report feeling as if they have more time (Mogilner et al. 2012). Time affluence has also been found to be related to positive subjective well-being, even after controlling for material affluence (Kasser and Sheldon 2009).

***

The "good life" has been broadened beyond terms of material or national affluence to include health, security, respect, friendship, leisure, and self-development. Research across thirty European countries confirms that such qualities have a positive effect on subjective well-being (Delhey and Steckermeier 2016). Forgeard and Seligman (2012) provide a review of research on the benefits of holding a "glass half full," flexible and realistic optimism, including greater happiness, health, and success. Greater optimism enables greater motivation and pursuit of goals, including better social relations (Carver and Scheier 2014).

***

In a meta-analysis of studies on spirituality and religiosity (S/R), Koenig (2012) found that S/R correlated with positive character traits (such as altruism, forgiveness, gratefulness, kindness, and compassion), as well as with a greater sense of personal control over stressful situations. S/R also correlated with less depression and anxiety, greater well-being, happiness, hope, optimism, meaning, and purpose, as well as better health practices and outcomes. Children's spirituality, but not religious practices, was found in one study to be linked to their level of happiness, paralleling the results of happiness studies of adults (Holder et al. 2008).

33. No-Self, No Target

The experience of feeling targeted, as by social rejection, has been found to activate the same brain pathways as activated in response to physical pain (Kross et al. 2007). Brain response to facial expressions conveying disapproval, anger, or disgust was measured using fMRI scans (Burklund et al. 2007). Participants who scored higher on rejection sensitivity demonstrated greater neural response to the disapproving faces.

A longitudinal study of defense mechanisms across adulthood in a European-American sample found that increases in ego level were associated with increased use of intellectualization as a defense (Diehl et al. 2014). More "adaptive" types of defenses (such as sublimation, suppression, and intellectualization vs. doubt, displacement, and regression) were found to be used in adulthood vs. in adolescence, but this trend reversed in old age.

***

The nonjudging component of mindfulness has been found to operate as a proactive factor for rejection sensitivity (Peters et al. 2016). Those high in ability to be mindful and nonjudging were found to experience less negative affect associated with rejection sensitivity.

A study of emotional stability in meditators found that those with more meditation experience demonstrated less physiologic reactivity to stimulation than novice meditators (Lee et al. 2015). A review of studies on compassion and loving-kindness meditation found them of significant benefit in improving interpersonal relations, empathic accuracy, positive affect, and positive thinking, as well as in decreasing psychological distress (Shonin et al. 2013).

A study of mindfulness, distress tolerance, and relationship violence in a sample of women found that those who were able to not judge or react to their inner experiences, but rather act with awareness (rather than criticism or avoidance), were better able to tolerate temporary distress and less likely to abuse a dating partner (Brem et al. 2016).

34. No-Self, No Aging

The majority of seniors studied report younger subjective age (how young individuals experience themselves to be) (Mirucka et al. 2016). Subjective age has been found to predict positive orientation and life satisfaction and also to be associated with self-esteem. Younger subjective age among older adults has been found to predict lower psychological distress as well as to mitigate the distress experienced by feeling closer to death (Shira et al. 2014).

***

An fMRI study of neural processing associated with linguistic death cues investigated the neural substrates underlying death-related thoughts (Liu et al. 2013). EEG recordings found an early modulation in response to death-related cues prior to emotional response, which was also associated with participants' level of dispositional pessimism. The early detection of death-cues may reflect an increased neurocognitive evaluation of death-thoughts compared to neutral or life-affirming ones.

***

Self-transcendence has been found to be negatively correlated with death anxiety (Baker 2009) and to be a predictor of successful aging (McCarthy et al. 2013). Self-transcendence has also been found to correlate strongly with sense of coherence, hope, self-esteem, and variables assessing emotional well-being (Coward 1996). Even among vulnerable populations, such as the homeless (Runquist and Reed 2007) or chronically ill (JadidMilani et al. 2015), self-transcendence has been correlated with health and well-being.

***

Near-death experiences have been reported across cultures throughout history, with 10 to 20 percent of people today who have come close to death reporting such an occurrence. The invariance in these reports, regardless of diverse cultures and contexts, suggests either a universal neurophysiological process, such as stimulation of temporal lobes (Blanke and Thut 2007), or a possible transcendent domain that challenges the concept of mind as a by-product of neural circuitry (Greyson 2015).

In most cases, people report qualities of peace, serenity, and acceptance after these near-death experiences (Konopka 2015), as well as an instantaneous and pervasive elimination of death fear (Tassell-Matamua and Lindsay 2016). Near-death experiences, including out-of-body phenomena, have also been associated with greater post-traumatic growth when compared to those who have had close brushes with death without the near-death mystical components (Khanna and Greyson 2015).

35. The Effectiveness Test

Selfless psychological functioning (defined as engaging flexibly and fluidly among dynamic, changing relations) has been theorized as a source of authentic, durable happiness. This model contrasts with the perception of a *structured self* (permanent, independent, and solid) that engages in self-centered psychological functioning and appears to be associated with fluctuating happiness (Dambrun and Ricard 2011).

Self-concept has been found to mediate perception of life satisfaction (Silvestre and Landa 2016) and quality of life ratings (Clare et al. 2013) in clinical and nonclinical samples. The relationship between identity regulation and health outcomes has been investigated, especially in terms of how self-regulation helps or hinders health-promoting behaviors (Shepperd et al. 2011). Conceptual selves, such as "the entrapped self" or "maintaining consistency of past self," have been found to affect patients' experience with chronic pain. Results highlight the value of fluidity in shaping a range of possible selves (Hellstrom 2001).

***

Expanded self-concept (not self-esteem) has been linked to greater self-efficacy (Mattingly and Lewandowski 2013). Research has also shown that when people define themselves as relational and interdependent, they report more satisfying friendships than those who score low in relational-interdependent self-construal (Boucher 2014). Studies have found that effort put forth in maintaining self-presentation with others who are close decreases relationship satisfaction (Gosnell et al. 2011).

Self-enhancement has been found to lead to increased satisfaction only when one's passions and actions are associated with an insecure sense of self (Lafreniere et al. 2013). For those who demonstrate secure sense of self and genuine passion toward an activity, no effect was found between self-enhancement and life satisfaction. Research has also found that discrepancies between one's actual and ideal personality are negatively correlated with purpose in life, with agency as a possible mediating variable (Stanley and Burrow 2015).

***

Researchers investigated the Eastern idea of nothingness and its relationship with people's well-being in Japan (Kan et al. 2009). They suggest that a "minimalist" conception of well-being founded on attention toward the fluidity, transience, and mystery of life enables people to experience gratitude and peaceful disengagement.

An orientation toward happiness that endorses engagement and flow has been found to predict satisfaction with life (Buschor et al. 2013). Research has found that daily savoring of positive experiences in the moment functions as a way to increase happiness (Jose et al. 2012).

***

The notion that humans are narrative in nature and that a narrative outlook is essential to a life well-lived has been challenged (Woods 2011). The limits of narrative have been explored in the medical humanities; the possibilities that exist beyond or in conjunction with narrative, such as metaphor and phenomenology, have also been explored (McKechnie 2014). Mindfulness, for example, has been called for during the process of physician-patient communication to carefully shape the treatment narrative and prevent reification of the patient's "story" (Connelly 2005).

36. Acting As If

The acting *as if* therapeutic technique, or role-playing, was developed a hundred years ago by physician and psychotherapist Alfred Adler. It continues to be a useful method today in cognitive behavioral therapy and other treatment modalities. The technique, for example, has been integrated with constructivist perspectives into the *as if* reflective process, helping clients access their imagination and creativity to co-construct and implement action plans based on who they would like to be (Watts et al. 2005; Watts 2003).

Active imagination, as introduced by Carl Jung and modified over the years into different psychotherapies, is a related technique to acting as if, engaging clients with the healing and visioning powers of the imaginal or transpersonal realm (Jung 1997).

Eye movement desensitization and reprocessing therapy is a research-based treatment for healing trauma that activates neural networks using imagination and bilateral stimulation. Clients come to feel physiologically "resourced" through the imagining of protective, nurturing, and wise figures in their lives and the visioning of alternative, idealized personal histories and futures (Parnell 2013).

Imaginative processes have been used in fields other than therapy. A fictional inquiry process, for instance, has been used in the arts that allows for exploration into the future of collaborative design (Dindler and Iversen 2007). Using fictional narratives to bypass existing sociocultural structures, fictional inquiry helps generate ideas and initiate organizational change. Imaginative cognition and use of conceptual experimentation has also contributed to discoveries in mathematics and science (e.g., Châtelet 1991).

The use of imagination has even been studied in its role in increasing body strength (in the absence of actual physical muscle-building tasks). Researchers have found that, without performing the physical exercise, mental training does in fact enhance cortical signals that activate muscles and build strength (Ranganathan et al. 2004). The effective mental training of competitive athletes with motor imagery has borne out these findings

(Schuster et al. 2011). Another application of motor imagery training facilitates the improvement of muscle activity in stroke victims (Oh and Choi 2017).

37. Smart Selfing

In a review of the literature, researchers have come to understand that the multiplicity of cognitions that constitute the self and the neural structures underlying them has developed as a human capacity through evolutionary selection (Skowronski and Sedikides 2017). Neuroscience has distinguished self from identity in terms of the former's association with right hemisphere, reflexive, nonlinguistic experience, and the latter with left hemisphere, reflective, verbally mediated experience (Gerson 2014).

***

Current models of identity development focus on the integrative nature of identity as contextualized, emergent, and continuous (Galliher et al. 2017). The dynamic systems model of role identity, for example, emphasizes identity as anchored in action and influenced by intra- and interpersonal processes (Kaplan and Garner 2017). Identity has also been described as a construction in response to external needs for self-identification (Monceri 2009). It has been linked to the way in which people organize self-defining memories and prospective thoughts together cognitively, which provides meaning to specific past and future life events (Demblon and D'Argembeau 2017).

Identity researchers have postulated that, in addition to internal dialogical activity, certain motivational goals drive identity construction: self-esteem, self-efficacy, continuity, distinctiveness, belonging, and meaning (Vignoles et al. 2006). When identity is experimentally threatened, the most distressing components involve potential loss of self-esteem and meaning (Batory 2015).

***

A series of studies found that expanded self-concept correlates with greater sense of self-efficacy (Mattingly and Lewandowski 2013). Even those who expand representations of their self-concepts, such as through the use of artistic rendering, report greater self-efficacy at resolving problems than those who do not physically expand their self-concept representations.

The expansion of self-concept has been found to have other benefits. Researchers have found that holding stereotypes about the elderly actually impairs the elderly's memory recall (Liu et al. 2017). But when older subjects are able to call upon multiple sources of identity (making their self-concept more robust), it buffers the stereotype threat effect on their memory performance.

The importance of clarity regarding self-concept was demonstrated in studies showing that such clarity mediates the relationship between stressful life events and subjective well-being (Ritchie et al. 2011). Interestingly, those who construe their self as stable and unchanging tend to suffer decreases in well-being and self-esteem when confronted with identity conflict (Rabinovich and Morton 2016). Those who perceive the self as flexible do not suffer such effects in the face of identity conflict.

***

The "mindful self" has been developed as a concept based on studies showing improvements in attitudes toward oneself with mindfulness practice (Xiao et al. 2017). Such an application of Buddhist psychology may serve as an intermediary between mindfulness and mental health problems and also promote well-being.

However, some criticisms target the use of mindfulness in the psychological sciences, noting how such applications ignore the foundational Buddhist views on personal identity (Panaioti 2015). They argue that, rather than continuing to compartmentalize Buddhist practices from Buddhist theory, Western beliefs about the self need to take into account these insights about cosmopolitan selfhood for a truly integrated and holistic approach.

38. Off the I-land

Researchers have found distinct subjective and physiological characteristics pertaining to different levels of self-awareness (Travis et al. 2004). Higher consciousness scores and more efficient cortical responses, for example, were found among those who defined themselves abstractly as an enduring self-sense underneath thoughts, feelings, and actions as opposed to the lower consciousness scores found among those defining themselves by their concrete thinking and behavioral processes.

***

One's cultural orientation, toward either individualism or collectivism, affects the importance of personality traits vs. the importance of social identity to one's sense of selfhood. The finding that collectivistic people tend to focus more on social identity (vs. personality traits) has also been borne out through neuroscience studies showing a differential activation pattern in the self-referencing parts of the brain of individualists (Sul et al. 2012).

One study on self-construal found stronger relationships between certain identity structures (identity valuation, stability, and coherence) and subjective well-being for those who have more of an independent self-construal (Pilarska 2014). In contrast, for those with more of an interdependent self-construal, relationships were weaker between these identity structures of uniqueness and subjective well-being.

***

The notion of collective identity has been explored within the social sciences, specifically how a shared sense of group belonging contributes to emotional investment among individuals, social movements, and international alliances (e.g., Snow and Corrigall-Brown 2015; Melucci 1995; Wendt 1994). More recently, a theory of macrocognition has been proposed, in which a skillful and goal-directed collective mentality can develop, allowing for collective intentionality and responsibility (Huebner 2014). The notion of collective identity has expanded beyond specific group allegiance toward a larger collective consciousness. For instance, "we-space" practices and communities have developed focusing on "we interconnectedness" vs. "I separateness" (Gunnlaugson and Brabant 2016).

***

Self-transcendence has been found to predict social and emotional competence (Athota et al. 2015). People who more strongly endorse self-transcendence values (e.g., having higher "humanity esteem") tend to show stronger *ecocentrism*, personal moral norms and behavioral intentions to protect the environment (Cheung et al. 2014).

Studies have shown that those engaged in a daily mindfulness-oriented meditation practice demonstrate greater characterological maturity at the intrapersonal (self-directedness), interpersonal (cooperativeness), and transpersonal (self-transcendence) levels (Campanella et al. 2014). In one study, participants in a multidimensional well-being program that included meditation, yoga, breathing practices, and emotional expression through journaling and emotional support demonstrated a significant and sustained shift in transpersonal self-awareness and identity compared to controls. The shift was measured using the validated Nondual Embodiment Thematic Inventory that assesses level of disidentification from the mind, propensity to surrender, interest in truth, and resilience, among other qualities (Mills et al. 2017).

Awareness of present experience has also been found to impact ethical decision making. Individuals high in mindfulness report a greater likelihood of acting ethically and upholding ethical standards. They have been found, for example, to cheat less in studies (Ruedy and Schweitzer 2010).

39. The No-Self Revolution

Language organizes the world symbolically. That the structure of language influences or even determines the speaker's worldview is a linguistic relativity theory known as Sapir-Whorf hypothesis (Koerner 1992). Reasoning strategies and discourse are often shaped by language whose heuristics are often determined by geography and culture (Vallverdu 2017).

Studies have shown that (1) repeated exposure to first-person singular pronouns (I, my, me, mine) primes an individualistic orientation compared to first-person plural pronoun exposure (we, our, us, ours), which primes a collectivist orientation; and (2) cultural orientation affects one's choice of pronouns, with those with a collectivist orientation preferring use of first-person plural possessive pronouns, compared to those individualistically oriented (Na and Choi 2009). Studies have found that those who score higher on narcissism use more first-person singular pronouns and fewer first-person plural pronouns (Raskin and Shaw 1988).

Neuroscientists measuring event-related brain potentials in participants visually exposed to personal and possessive self-referential pronouns ("I" and "my") found that such stimuli were spontaneously processed preferentially compared to non-self-referential pronouns ("he/his") (Blume and Herbert 2014). Additional attention was also found to be allocated to the self-referential pronouns at later stage processing. Researchers call this the HisMine-paradigm, finding that stimuli related to oneself benefits from early differential neurological processing.

Experiments demonstrate that varying the pronouns in a narrative affects the embodiment experienced by the reader during comprehension. Readers tend to take on the actor's perspective when the first-person "I" is used vs. taking on an external onlooker perspective via pronouns like "he" or "she" (Brunye et al. 2009). Brain fMRIs reveal that different neural networks are activated when third- or first-person pronouns are used referencing a protagonist in a written narrative (Hartung et al. 2017). Researchers conclude that comprehension is dependent upon linguistically encoded perspective.

A new language, Toki Pona, has been developed by linguist and translator Sonja Lang, inspired by Taoism to shape the conceptual process of its speakers toward a "simple and honest life," immersed in the present moment with a propensity toward positivity (Lang 2014). Pronouns in this language are limited and do not denote gender or number ("he," "she," "it," and "they" are all signified by the same word).

***

Evolutionary developmental models for prosocial behavior note the biological bases for prosocial behavior early in life. Yet this emergence is affected by whether environmental support, expectations, and social norms exist for prosocial behavior (per social learning theory) (O'Brien 2014). Individual development has been specifically theorized as influenced by and bifurcated along a continuum of individualist and collectivists cultures (Castrechini-Franieck 2016).

In Western societies with independent self-construal, an endowment effect has been found among children three to four years of age in which possessions take on an "extended self" significance or value, reflecting an early conditioning of attentional self-bias (Hood et al. 2016).

***

Arrested personal development is discussed by psychologist Bill Plotkin (2008), especially as it relates to an industrial growth society that alienates humanity from nature, resulting in an "immature citizenry" unable to develop beyond adolescence.

An evolutionary psychopathological framework for narcissism has been proposed that accounts for the increases in narcissism in Western, individualist cultures (Szekeres and Tisljar 2013). Social scientists have discussed the effect of contemporary corporate culture in distancing people from their essential environmental and interpersonal connectedness, and the resulting "manic defenses" that have developed, such as excessive shopping designed to fill the emotional void of what has been lost (Rudan et al. 2016).

The perception of American national culture has been investigated by researchers with the finding that American adults perceive Americans in general as more narcissistic, disagreeable, and antisocial than they perceive themselves individually (Miller et al. 2015). A world sample rated Americans as more extroverted, antagonistic, and narcissistic than members of their own countries.

A nationwide meta-analysis of college students' scores on the Narcissistic Personality Inventory shows significant increases in rates of the syndrome from 1982 to 2008 (Twenge and Foster 2010). A cultural syndrome of "vertical individualism" has been found to be negatively associated with self-transcendence and positively associated with immature love (Le and Levenson 2005).

***

Indices other than gross domestic product have been used to evaluate countries' progress. For instance, the gross national happiness (GNH) appraisal, inspired by a national happiness philosophy introduced by the King of Bhutan in 1972, includes assessment of nine development areas including equity and sustainability, both economically and environmentally (Metz 2014). Gross national well-being (GNW), published in 2005 by the International Institute of Management (IIM), is a secular model for assessing socioeconomic development that examines such development across the following seven dimensions: work; social, political, mental, environmental, and physical well-being; and satisfaction (IIM 2005). The GNW is seen as a second generation GNH designed to bridge the gap between Western objective socioeconomic policy and holistic, subjective Eastern philosophy-based measures.

The US Environmental Protection Agency has also developed a metric, Human Wellbeing Index (HWBI), to evaluate the influence of social, economic, and environmental impact on sustainable human well-being using eight domains weighted by relative importance (Smith et al. 2012). In addition, the Social Progress Imperative developed a Social Progress Index (SPI) that ranks countries on a range of social and environmental indicators along three core dimensions: opportunity, basic human needs, and well-being (Porter and Stern 2017). While findings do indicate a correlation between GDP and higher SPI score, a country's income often does not correspond to its level of social progress.

***

Notable gains have been made in the movement for nonhuman personhood legal rights and protections (Dvorsky 2014). The definition of personhood is under debate, with proposed updates spanning the inclusion of select species of animals to whole ecosystems. New systems models argue for a modified humanism, revised to eliminate boundaries between humans and the environment (Midgley 1994).

A demographic study investigating public attitudes toward forests and environmental attitudes in general found that a biocentric orientation is favored by a younger versus older generation, suggesting to some possible emergence of a postmaterial society (Tarrant and Cordell 2002).

***

Science historians have noted that revolutionary paradigm shifts have occurred over the ages as a result of various factors, including not only technological discoveries in science but also conceptual advances as well (Casadevall and Fang 2016). Serendipity, inspiration, and convergence of anomalous observations all factor into what creates a transformative scientific revolution.

Researchers suggest that an integral spirituality is emerging, fueled by the synthesis of scientific currents into an integral science (Gulick 2004). In addition, the current biopsychosocial model of the human being in health sciences has been called upon to expand to the biopsychosocial-spiritual model. The multifaceted nature of "spiritual" has been clarified in order to promote such a paradigm shift in medicine (Saad et al. 2017).

Claims of a spiritual revolution in Britain were analyzed using national survey data assessing presence of alternative spirituality in the general culture relative to institutional religion (Glendinning and Bruce 2006). The need for a global spiritual awakening is also discussed by King (2011), with a spiritual oneness of humanity as the agent of personal and social change.

Acknowledgments

I would like to acknowledge the generous people who made this book possible. First, I value and thank the many clients I have worked with in individual therapy, group psychotherapy, and the classes I have taught over the years. I admire their courage, insight, and integrity. I've been deeply moved by our work together and by the privilege of getting to know their truest self and no-self, which has inspired material for this book.

I am very grateful for the loving encouragement of my husband, Jonathan Gustin, during the long process of manifesting *The No-Self Help Book*. I thank him for his tireless support of me through many rounds of neurotic *selfing* on this project and his example of being an agent of cultural change in the world.

I am also thankful to my dharma brothers and sisters—Gwen Weil, Dave Schultz, David Michelson, Denise Turner—for their feedback on early drafts of *The No-Self Help Book* and for helping to keep the morale going. Their wisdom and guidance have shaped the book (and my life) toward a fuller, deeper expression. I'd also like to acknowledge my parents for helping install the important values of learning and truth-seeking, science and study, into my upbringing.

Other friends and colleagues also offered support and interest in *The No-Self Help Book* vital to the book's completion. I am most grateful for the kindness and generous spirit of Dan and Belinda Lyons Newman, Suzanne Eaves, Simone Rodin, Tracye Williams, Julie Fennimore, Michelle Fontaine, and the ladies of the meditation group.

Much gratitude goes to Byron Belitsos for his assistance with the initial book proposal and directing me to Non-Duality Press/New Harbinger Publications, toward whom I cannot offer enough praise. Thank you to my editor, Elizabeth Hollis Hansen, for going to bat for this unusual text, and to my copyeditor, Jean Blomquist, for her amazing attention to detail, and to the whole team at New Harbinger for being so skilled at what they do. I am also grateful for the generous contributions of those who have endorsed *The No-Self Help Book*.

I am indebted to many wise souls for their spiritual instruction. The presence and teachings of Adyashanti, Rupert Spira, Byron Katie, Eckhart Tolle, and Candice O'Denver have been profoundly impactful on me, to name a few. My appreciation also goes to Eleanor Rosch for her graduate seminar, Clinical Applications of Eastern Thought, at UC Berkeley twenty-five years ago, for providing me with a first doorway into the overlapping realms of dharma and psychology.

Finally, I am grateful for the greatest teacher of all, my son, who reminds me daily of the irrepressible joy, delight, and exuberance possible when living as no-self.

References

Abel, E., and M. Kruger. 2010. Smile intensity in photographs predicts longevity. *Psychological Science* 21, 4: 542–44.

Ahrens, C. J. C., C. J. Chrouser, and C. D. Ryff. 2006. Multiple roles and well-being: Sociodemographic and psychological moderators. *Sex Roles* 55: 801–15.

Aknin, L. B., C. P. Barrington-Leigh, E. W. Dunn, J. F. Helliwell, J. Burns, R. Biswas-Diener, I. Kemeza, P. Nyende, and C. E. Ashton-James. 2013. Prosocial spending and well-being: Cross-cultural evidence for a psychological universal. *Journal of Personality and Social Psychology* 104, 4: 635–52.

Aknin, L. B., J. K. Hamlin, and E. W. Dunn. 2012. Giving leads to happiness in young children. *PLoS ONE* 7, 6: e39211. doi:10.1371/journal.pone.0039211.

Akutsu, S., A. Yamaguchi, M. S. Kim, and A. Oshio. 2016. Self-construals, anger regulation, and life satisfaction in the United States and Japan. *Frontiers in Psychology* 31, 7: 768.

Alderson-Day, B., S. Weis, S. McCarthy-Jones, P. Moseley, D. Smailes, and C. Fernyhough. 2016. The brain's conversations with itself: Neural substrates of dialogic inner speech. *Social Cognitive and Affective Neuroscience* 11, 1: 110–20.

Allman, M. J., S. Teki, T. D. Griffiths, and W. H. Meck. 2014. Properties of the internal clock: First- and second-order principles of subjective time. *Annual Review of Psychology* 65: 743–71.

Al-Namiah, A., E. S. Meins, and C. Fernyhough. 2012. Self-regulatory private speech relates to children's recall and organization of autobiographical memories. *Early Childhood Research Quarterly* 27, 3: 441–46.

Alter, A. L., and D. Oppenheimer. 2006. Predicting short-term stock fluctuations by using processing fluency. *Proceedings of the National Academy of Sciences* 103, 24: 9369–72.

Anselme, P., and M. J. F. Robinson. 2016. "Wanting," "liking," and their relation to consciousness. *Journal of Experimental Psychology* 42, 2: 123–40.

Arch, J. J., K. W. Brown, R. J. Goodman, M. D. Della Porta, L. G. Kiken, and S. Tilman. 2016. Enjoying food without caloric cost: The impact of brief mindfulness on laboratory eating outcomes. *Behaviour Research and Therapy* 79: 23–34.

Aspinwall, L. G., and S. E. Taylor. 1993. Effects of social comparison direction, threat, and self-esteem on affect, self-evaluation, and expected success. *Journal of Personality and Social Psychology* 64, 5: 708–22.

Assor, A., G. Roth, and E. L. Deci. 2004. The emotional costs of parents' conditional regard: A self-determination theory analysis. *Journal of Personality* 72, 1: 47–88.

Athota, V. S., S. P. Kearney, and E. Cocodia. 2015. How self-transcendence via individualized moral foundations predict emotional and social enhancement. *Journal of Beliefs & Values: Studies in Religion & Education* 36, 3: 297–307.

Atwood, J. D., and L. Maltin. 1991. Putting Eastern philosophies into Western psychotherapies. *American Journal of Psychotherapy* 45, 3: 368–82.

Avni-Badad, D., and I. Ritov. 2003. Routine and the perception of time. *Journal of Experimental Psychology: General* 132, 4: 543–50.

Avinun, R., S. Israel, I. Shalev, I. Gritsenko, G. Bornstein, and R. P. Ebstein. 2011. AVPR1A variant associated with preschoolers' lower altruistic behavior. *PLoS ONE* 6, 9: e25274.

Baker, B. 2009. Relationship of self-transcendence and death anxiety to older adult's participation in health promotion behavior. *Southern Online Journal of Nursing Research* 9, 2: 1.

Baltes, P. B., and K. U. Mayer, eds. 1999. *The Berlin Aging Study: Aging from 70 to 100.* Cambridge, UK: Cambridge University Press.

Batory, A. M. 2015. What self-aspects appear significant when identity is in danger? Motives crucial under identity threat. *Journal of Constructivist Psychology* 28, 2: 166–80.

Baumeister, R. F., and J. Tierney. 2012. *Willpower: Rediscovering the Greatest Human Strength.* New York: Penguin Books.

Baumgartner, T., M. Heinrichs, A. Volanthen, U. Fischbacher, and E. Fehr. 2008. Oxytocin shapes the neural circuitry of trust and trust adaptation in humans. *Neuron* 58, 4: 639–50.

Beauregard, M., J. Courtemanche, V. Paquette, and E. L. St. Pierre. 2009. The neural basis of unconditional love. *Psychiatry Research* 172, 2: 93–98.

Berenson, K. R., and G. Downey. 2006. Self-esteem and rejection sensitivity in close relationships. In M. Kernis (ed.), *Self-Esteem: Issues and Answers,* 367–74. New York: Psychology Press.

Bernstein, M. J., S. G. Young, C. M. Brown, D. F. Sacco, and H. M. Claypool. 2008. Adaptive responses to social exclusion: Social rejection improves detection of real and fake smiles. *Psychological Science* 19, 10: 981–83.

Blanke, O., and G. Thut. 2007. Inducing out-of-body experiences. In Sergio Della Sala (ed.), *Tall Tales: Separating Fact from Fiction,* 425–49. Oxford, UK: Oxford University Press.

Block, J., and J. H. Block. 2006. Nursery school personality and political orientation two decades later. *Journal of Research in Personality* 40, 5: 734–39.

Block, R. A., P. A. Hancock, and D. Zackay. 2010. How cognitive load affects duration judgments: A meta-analytic review. *Acta Psychologica* 134, 3: 330–43.

Blom, V. 2012. Contingent self-esteem, stressors, and burnout in working men and women. *Work* 43, 2: 123–31.

Blume, C., and C. Herbert. 2014. The HisMine-paradigm: A new paradigm to investigate self-awareness employing pronouns. *Social Neuroscience* 9, 3: 289–99.

Boucher, H. C. 2014. The relational-interdependent self-construal and positive illusions in friendship. *Self and Identity* 13, 4: 460–76.

Bourgeois K. S., and M. R. Leary. 2001. Coping with rejection: Derogating those who choose us last. *Motivation and Emotion* 25, 2: 101–11.

Brambilla, M., and C. W. Leach. 2014. On the importance of being moral: The distinctive role of morality in social judgment. *Social Cognition* 32, 4: 397–408.

Braslow, M. D., J. Geurrettaz, R. M. Arkin, and K. C. Oleson. 2012. Self-doubt. *Social and Personality Psychology Compass* 6, 6: 470–82.

Brem, M. J., A. Khaddouma, J. Elmquist, A. R. Florimbio, R. C. Shorey, and G. L. Stuart. 2016. Relationships among dispositional mindfulness, distress tolerance, and women's dating violence perpetration: A path analysis. *Journal of Interpersonal Violence* (August): doi:10.1177/0886260516664317.

Brickman, P., and D. T. Campbell. 1971. Hedonic relativism and planning the good society. In M. H. Apley (ed.), *Adaptation Level Theory: A Symposium*, 287–302. New York: Academic Press.

Brickman, P., D. Coates, and R. Janoff-Bulman. 1978. Lottery winners and accident victims: Is happiness relative? *Journal of Personality and Social Psychology* 36, 8: 917–27.

Brody, G. H., and X. Ge. 2001. Linking parenting processes and self-regulation to psychological functioning and alcohol use in early adolescence. *Journal of Family Psychology* 15, 1: 82–94.

Brotto, L. A., and R. Basson. 2014. Group mindfulness-based therapy significantly improves sexual desire in women. *Behaviour Research and Therapy* 57: 43–54.

Brown, S. L., D. M. Smith, R. Schultz, M. U. Kabeto, P. A. Ubel, M. Pulin, J. Yi, C. Kim, and K. M. Langa. 2009. Caregiving behavior is associated with decreased mortality risk. *Psychological Science* 20, 4: 488–94.

Brummelman, E., S. Thomaes, G. Overbeek, B. Orobio de Castro, M. A. van den Hout, and B. J. Bushman. 2013. On feeding those hungry for praise: Person praise backfires in children with low self-esteem. *Journal of Experimental Psychology: General* 143, 1: 9–14. doi:10.1037/a0031917.

Brunye, T. T., T. Ditman, C. R. Mahoney, J. S. Augustyn, and H. A. Taylor. 2009. When you and I share perspectives: Pronouns modulate perspective taking during narrative comprehension. *Psychological Science* 20, 1: 27–32.

Bshary, R., and N. J. Raihani. 2017. Helping in humans and other animals: A fruitful interdisciplinary dialogue. *Proceedings of the Royal Society B: Biological Sciences* 284, 1863. doi:10.1098/rspb.2017.0929.

Burklund, L. J., N .I. Eisenberger, and M. D. Lieberman. 2007. The face of rejection: Rejection sensitivity moderates dorsal anterior cingulate activity to disapproving facial expressions. *Social Neuroscience* 2, 3–4: 238–53.

Buschor, C., R. T. Proyer, and W. Ruch. 2013. Self- and peer-rated character strengths: How do they relate to satisfaction with life and orientation to happiness? *Journal of Positive Psychology* 8, 2: 116–27.

Bushman, B. J. 2002. Does venting anger feed or extinguish the flame? Catharsis, rumination, distraction, anger, and aggressive responding. *Personality and Social Psychology Bulletin* 28, 6: 724–31.

Bushman, B. J., S. J. Moeller, S. Konrath, and J. Crocker. 2012. Investigating the link between liking versus wanting self-esteem and depression in a nationally representative sample of American adults. *Journal of Personality* 80, 5: 1453–69.

Cameron, N. 2015. Is it time for a whine detox? *Good Health* (Australian edition), December, 60–61.

Campanella, F., C. Crescentini, C. Urgesi, and F. Fabbro. 2014. Mindfulness-oriented meditation improves self-related character scales in healthy individuals. *Comprehensive Psychiatry* 55, 5: 1269–78.

Carr, E. W., S. Korb, P. M. Niedenthal, and P. Winkielman. 2014. The two sides of spontaneity: Movement onset asymmetries in facial expression influence social judgments. *Journal of Experimental Social Psychology* 55: 31–36.

Carver, C. S., and M. F. Scheier. 2014. Dispositional optimism. *Trends in Cognitive Science* 18, 6: 293–99.

Casadevall, A., and F. C. Fang. 2016. Revolutionary science. *MBio* 7, 2: e00158.

Castrechini-Franieck, M. L. 2016. Remarks on latency: Onset in different cultures. *Journal of Psychohistory* 43, 3: 214–27.

Chandler, J. J. 2012. Fast thought speed induces risk taking. *Psychological Science* 23, 4: 370–74.

Chang, L. C., and R. M. Arkin. 2002. Materialism as an attempt to cope with uncertainty. *Psychology and Marketing* 19, 5: 389–406.

Chang, R. S., and N. S. Thompson. 2010. The attention-getting capacity of whines and child-directed speech. *Evolutionary Psychology* 8, 2: 260–74.

———. 2011. Whines, cries, and motherese: Their relative power to distract. *Evolutionary Behavioral Sciences* 5, 2: 131–41.

Chaplin, L. N., and D. R. John. 2007. Growing up in a material world: Age differences in materialism in children and adolescents. *Journal of Consumer Research* 34, 4: 480–93.

Châtelet, G. 1991. *Figuring Space: Philosophy, Mathematics, and Physics.* Dordrecht, Netherlands: Kluer Academic Publishers.

Chavez, R. S., and T. F. Heatherton. 2014. Multimodal frontostriatal connectivity underlies individual differences in self-esteem. *Social Cognitive and Affective Neuroscience* 10, 3: 364–70.

Chen, C. C., P. Saparito, and L. Belkin. 2011. Responding to trust breaches: The domain specificity of trust and the role of affect. *Journal of Trust Research* 1, 1: 85–106.

Cheung, W. L., M. A. Luke, and G. R. Maio. 2014. On attitudes towards humanity and climate change: The effects of humanity esteem and self-transcendence values on environmental concerns. *European Journal of Social Psychology* 44, 5: 496–506.

Chomsky, N. 2000. *New Horizons in the Study of Language and Mind.* Cambridge, UK: Cambridge University Press.

Christoff, K., D. Cosmelli, D. Legrand, and E. Thompson. 2011. Specifying the self for cognitive neuroscience. *Trends in Cognitive Science* 15, 3: 104–22.

Christov-Moore, L., T. Sugiyama, K. Grigaiyte, and M. Iacoboni. 2017. Increasing generosity by disrupting prefrontal cortex. *Social Neuroscience* 12, 2: 174–81.

Cialdini, R. B., S. L. Brown, B. P. Lewis, C. Luce, and S. L. Neuberg. 1997. Reinterpreting the empathy-altruism relationship: When one into one equals oneness. *Journal of Personality and Social Psychology* 73, 3: 481–91.

Cicirelli, V. G. 2002. Fear of death in older adults: Predictions from terror management theory. *Journals of Gerontology, Series B,* 57, 4: 358–66.

Cisek, S. Z., C. Sedikides, C. M. Hart, H. J. Godwin, V. Benson, and S. P. Liversedge. 2014. Narcissism and consumer behavior: A review and preliminary findings. *Frontiers in Psychology* 5: 232. doi:org/10.3389/fpsyg.2014.00232.

Clance, P. R., and S. A. Imes. 1978. The imposter phenomenon in high achieving women: Dynamics and therapeutic intervention. *Psychotherapy: Theory, Research, and Practice* 15, 3: 241–47.

Clapp. J. D., S. C. Patton, and J. G. Beck. 2015. Expressive inhibition in response to stress: Implications for emotional processing following trauma. *Journal of Anxiety Disorders* 29: 109–18.

Clare, L., C. J. Whitaker, S. M. Nelis, A. Martyr, I. S. Markova, I. Roth, R. T. Woods, and R. G. Morris. 2013. Self-concept in early stage dementia: Profile, course, correlates, predictors, and implications for quality of life. *International Journal of Geriatric Psychiatry* 28, 5: 494–503.

Clark, M., and K. Calleja. 2008. Shopping addiction: A preliminary investigation among Maltese university students. *Addiction Research and Theory* 16, 633–49.

Clark, M., K. Vardeman, and S. Barba. 2014. Perceived inadequacy: A study of the imposter phenomenon among college and research librarians. *College & Research Libraries* 75, 3: 255–71.

Cleck, J. N., and J. A. Blendy. 2008. Making a bad thing worse: Adverse effects of stress on drug addiction. *Journal of Clinical Investigation* 118, 2: 454–61.

Cohen, G. L., and D. K. Sherman. 2014. The psychology of change: Self-affirmation and social psychological intervention. *Annual Review of Psychology* 65: 333–71.

Cohen, S. S., S. Henin, and L. C. Parra. 2017. Engaging narratives evoke similar neural activity and lead to similar time perception. *Science Reports* 7, 1: 4578. doi:10.1038/s41598-017-04402-4.

Connelly, J. E. 2005. Narrative possibilities: Using mindfulness in clinical practice. *Perspectives in Biology and Medicine* 48, 1: 84–94.

Cosden, M. A., H. C. Ellis, and D. M. Feeney. 1979. Cognitive flexibility-rigidity, repetition effects, and memory. *Journal of Research in Personality* 13, 4: 386–95.

Costa Jr, P. T., A. Weiss, P. R. Duberstein, B. Friedman, and I. C. Siegler. 2014. Personality facets and all-cause mortality among Medicare patients aged 66 to 102 years: A follow-up of Weiss and Costs (2005). *Psychosomatic Medicine* 76, 5: 370–78.

Costa, R. M., T. F. Oliveira, J. Pestana, and D. Costa. 2016. Self-transcendence is related to higher female sexual desire. *Personality and Individual Differences* 96: 191–97.

Courage, M. L., S. Edison, and M. L. Howe. 2004. Variability in the early development of visual self-recognition. *Infant Behavior and Development* 27, 4: 509–32.

Coward, D. D. 1996. Self-transcendence and correlates in a healthy population. *Nursing Research* 45, 2: 116–21.

Crocker, J. 2002. The costs of seeking self-esteem. *Journal of Social Issues* 58, 3: 597–615.

Csikszentmihalyi, M. 2010. Effortless attention in everyday life: A systematic phenomenology. In B. Bruya (ed.), *Effortless Attention: A New Perspective in the Cognitive Science of Attention and Action*, 179–89. Cambridge, MA: MIT Press.

Curtis, S. C. 2016. The experience of self/no-self in aikido. *Journal of Consciousness Studies*, 23, 1–2: 58–68.

Damasio, A. R. 1999. *The Feeling of What Happens: Body and Emotion in the Making of Consciousness.* New York: Harcourt Brace.

Dambrun, M., and M. Ricard. 2011. Self-centeredness and selflessness: A theory of self-based psychological functioning and its consequences for happiness. *Review of General Psychology* 15, 2: 138–57.

Daniels, J. P., and M. von der Ruhr. 2010. Trust in others: Does religion matter? *Review of Social Economy* 68, 2: 163–86.

Danielsson, M., and H. Bengtsson. 2016. Global self-esteem and the processing of positive information about the self. *Personality and Individual Differences* 99: 325–30.

Dauenheimer, D. G., D. Stahlberg, S. Spreemann, and C. Sedikides. 2002. Self-enhancement, self-verification, or self-assessment: The intricate role of trait modifiability in the self-evaluation process. *Revue internationale de psychologie sociale* 15, 3–4: 89–112.

Delhey, J., and L. C. Steckermeier. 2016. The good life, affluence, and self-reported happiness: Introducing the Good Life Index and debunking two popular myths. *World Development* 88, C: 50–66.

Demblon, J., and A. D'Argembeau. 2017. Contribution of past and future self-defining event networks to personal identity. *Memory* 25, 5: 656–65.

Demo, D. H. 1992. The self-concept over time: Research issues and directions. *Annual Review of Sociology* 18: 303–26.

Denson, T. F., W. C. Pedersen, J. Ronquillo, and A. S. Nandy. 2008. The angry brain: Neural correlates of anger, angry rumination, and aggressive personality. *Journal of Cognitive Neuroscience* 21, 4: 734–44.

Diehl, M., H. Chui, E. L. Hay, M. A. Lumley, D. Gruhn, and G. Labouvie-Vief. 2014. Change in coping and defense mechanisms across adulthood: Longitudinal findings in a European-American sample. *Developmental Psychology* 50, 2: 634–48.

Dindler, C., and O. S. Iversen. 2007. Fictional inquiry: Design collaboration in a shared narrative space. *CoDesign: International Journal of CoCreation in Design and the Arts* 3, 4: 213–34.

Dougherty, D. D., S. L. Rauch, T. Deckersbach, C. Marci, R. Loh, L. M. Shin, N. M. Alpert, A. J. Fischman, and M. Fava. 2004. Ventromedial prefrontal cortex and amygdala dysfunction during an anger induction positron emission tomography study in patients with major depressive disorder with anger attacks. *Archives of General Psychiatry* 61, 8: 795–804.

Droit-Volet, S. 2013. Time perception in children: A neurodevelopmental approach. *Neuropsychologia* 51, 2: 220–34.

Droit-Volet, S., M. Fanget, and M. Dambrun. 2015. Mindfulness meditation and relaxation training increases time sensitivity. *Consciousness and Cognition* 31 (January): 86–97.

Duncan, L. E., and B. E. Peterson. 2014. Authoritarianism, cognitive rigidity, and the processing of ambiguous visual information. *Journal of Social Psychology* 154, 6: 480–90.

Duncan, L. G., J. D. Coatsworth, and M. T. Greenberg. 2009. A model of mindful parenting: Implications for parent-child relationships and prevention research. *Clinical and Child Family Psychology Review* 12, 3: 255–70.

Dunkley, C. R., K. M. Goldsmith, and B. B. Gorzalka. 2015. The potential role of mindfulness in protecting against sexual insecurities. *Canadian Journal of Human Sexuality* 24, 2: 92–103.

Dvorsky, G. 2014. The struggle for nonhuman personhood. *Journal of Evolution and Technology* 24, 3: 1–3.

Ekman, P., R. J. Davidson, and W. V. Friesen. 1990. The Duchenne smile: Emotional expression and brain physiology II. *Journal of Personality and Social Psychology* 58, 2: 342–53.

Emavardhana, T., and C. D. Tori. 1997. Changes in self-concept, ego defense mechanisms, and religiosity following seven-day Vipassana meditation retreats. *Journal for the Scientific Study of Religion* 36, 2: 194–206.

Esch, T., and G. B. Stefano. 2005a. The neurobiology of love. *Neuro Endocrinology Letters* 26, 3: 175–92.

———. 2005b. Love promotes health. *Neuro Endocrinology Letters* 26, 3: 264–67.

Everett, J. A., D. A. Pizarro, and M. J. Crockett. 2016. Inference of trustworthiness from intuitive moral judgments. *Journal of Experimental Psychology: General* 145, 6: 772–87.

Eysenck, M. W. 1990. *Happiness: Facts and Myths*. New York: Lawrence Erlbaum.

Faber, R., and T. O'Guinn. 1992. A clinical screener for compulsive buying. *Journal of Consumer Research* 19 (December): 459–69.

Fadjukoff, P., L. Pulkinen, A. L. Lyyra, and K. Kokko. 2016. Parental identity and its relation to parenting and psychological functioning in middle age. *Parenting Science and Practice* 16, 2: 87–107.

Falk, E. B., M. B. O'Donnell, C. N. Cascio, F. Tinney, Y. Kang, M. D. Lieberman, S. E. Taylor, L. An, K. Resnicow, and V. J. Strecher. 2015. Self-affirmation alters the brain's response to health messages and subsequent behavior change. *Proceedings of the National Academy of Sciences* 112, 7: 1977–82.

Feng, Z., A. Vlachantoni, X. Liu, and K. Jones. 2016. Social trust, interpersonal trust, and self-rated health in China: A multilevel study. *International Journal for Equity in Health* 15, 1: 180.

Ferguson, M. A., J. A. Nielsen, J. B. King, L. Dai, D. M. Giangrasso, R. Holman, J. R. Korenberg, and J. S. Anderson. 2016. Reward, salience, and attentional networks are activated by religious experience in devout Mormons. *Social Neuroscience* 13, 1: 104–116.

Fineman, N. R., L. Beckwith, J. Howard, and M. Espinosa. 1997. Maternal ego development and mother-infant interaction in drug-abusing women. *Journal of Substance Abuse and Treatment* 14, 4: 307–17.

Fingelkurts, A. A. 2009. Is our brain hardwired to produce God, or is our brain hardwired to perceive God? A systematic review on the role of the brain in mediating religious experience. *Cognitive Processes* 10, 4: 293–326.

Fiske, S. T., A. J. C. Cuddy, and P. Glick. 2007. Universal dimensions of social cognition: Warmth and competence. *Trends in Cognitive Sciences* 11, 2: 77–83.

Fivush, R. 2011. The development of autobiographical memory. *Annual Review of Psychology* 62: 559–82.

Forgas, J. P., and G. H. Bower. 1987. Mood effects on person-perception judgments. *Journal of Personality of Social Psychology* 53, 1: 53–60.

Forgeard, M. J. C., and M. E. P. Seligman. 2012. Seeing the glass half full: A review of the causes and consequences of optimism. *Pratiques Psychologiques* 18, 2: 107–20.

Fortner, B. V., and R. A. Neimeyer. 1999. Death anxiety in older adults: A quantitative review. *Death Studies* 23, 5: 387–411.

Fossati, P., S. J. Hevenor, M. Lepage, S. J. Graham, M. L. Keightley, F. Craik, and H. Mayberg. 2004. Distributed self in episodic memory: Neural correlates of successful retrieval of self-encoded positive and negative personality traits. *NeuroImage* 22, 4: 1596–1604.

Frederiksen, E. 2014. Relational trust: Outline of a Bourdieusian theory of interpersonal trust. *Journal of Trust Research* 4, 2: 167–92.

Freeman, J. B., R. M. Stolier, Z. A. Ingbretsen, and E. A. Hehman. 2014. Amygdala responsivity to high-level social information from unseen faces. *Journal of Neuroscience* 34, 32: 10573–81.

Frith, C. D., S. J. Blakemore, and D. M. Wolpert. 2000. Abnormalities in the awareness and control of action. *Philosophical Transactions of the Royal Society of London, Series B, Biological Sciences* 355, 1404: 1771–88.

Frith, U., and C. D. Frith. 2003. Development and neurophysiology of mentalizing. *Philosophical Transactions of the Royal Society of London, Series B, Biological Sciences* 358, 1431: 459–73.

Fugita, K., Y. Trope, N. Liberman, and M. Levin-Sagi. 2006. Construal levels and self-control. *Journal of Personality and Social Psychology* 90, 3: 351–67.

Gallagher, H. L., and C. D. Frith. 2003. Functional imaging of "Theory of Mind." *Trends in Cognitive Science* 7, 2: 77–83.

Gallagher, S. 2000. Philosophical conceptions of the self: Implications for cognitive science. *Trends in Cognitive Science* 4, 1: 14–21.

Galliher, R. V., K. C. McLean, and M. Syed. 2017. An integrated developmental model for studying identity content in context. *Developmental Psychology* 53, 11: 2011–22.

Garfield, A. M., B. B. Drwecki, C. F. Moore, K. V. Kortenkamp, and M. D. Gracz. 2014. The oneness beliefs scale: Connecting spirituality with proenvironmental behavior. *Journal for the Scientific Study of Religion* 53, 2: 356–72.

Germine, M. 1997. The physiology of collective consciousness. *World Futures* 48, 1–4: 57–104.

Gerson, M. 2014. Reconsidering self and identity through a dialogue between neuroscience and psychoanalytic theory. *Psychoanalytic Dialogues: The International Journal of Relational Perspectives* 24, 2: 210–26.

Gibran, Kahil. 1923. *The Prophet*. New York: Alfred Knopf.

Glendinning, T., and S. Bruce. 2006. New ways of believing or belonging: Is religion giving way to spirituality? *British Journal of Sociology* 57, 3: 399–414.

Gosnell, C. L., T. W. Britt, and E. S. Mckibben. 2011. Self-presentation in everyday life: Effort, closeness, and satisfaction. *Self and Identity* 10, 1: 18–31.

Gratton, A., and R. M. Sullivan. 2005. Role of prefrontal cortex in stress responsivity. In T. Steckler, N. H. Kalin, and J. M. H. M. Reul (eds.), *Handbook of Stress and the Brain*, vol. 1, 807–15. Dusseldorf, Germany: Elsevier.

Gravel, K., A. Deslauriers, M. Watiez, M. Dumont, A. A. Dufour Bouchard, and V. Provencher. 2014. Sensory-based nutrition pilot intervention for women. *Journal of the Academy of Nutrition and Dietetics* 114, 1: 99–106.

Greenberg, J., K. Reiner, and N. Meiran. 2012. "Mind the trap": Mindfulness practice reduces cognitive rigidity. *PLoS ONE* 7, 5: e36206.

Greenberg, J., S. Solomon, and T. Pyszczynski. 1997. Terror management theory of self-esteem and cultural worldviews: Empirical assessments and conceptual refinements. In M. P. Zanna (ed.), *Advances in Experimental Social Psychology*, vol. 29, 61–139. San Diego, CA: Academic Press.

Greyson, B. 2015. Western scientific approaches to near-death experiences. *Humanities* 4, 4: 775–96.

Gruenewald, T. L., D. H. Liao, and T. E. Seeman. 2012. Contributing to others, contributing to oneself: Perceptions of generativity and health in later life. *Journals of Gerontology, Series B*, 67, 6: 660–65.

Guggisberg, A. G., and A. Mottaz. 2013. Timing and awareness of movement decisions: Does consciousness really come too late? *Frontiers of Human Neuroscience* 7: 385. doi:10.3389/fnhum.2013.00385.

Gulick, D. S. 2004. The evolution of spiritual consciousness: Interface between integral science and spirituality, past and emerging. *World Futures: The Journal of New Paradigm Research* 60, 4: 335–41.

Gunnlaugson, O. and M. Brabant, eds. 2016. *Cohering the Integral We Space*. United States: Integral Publishing House.

Gyurak, A., C. I. Hooker, A. Miyakawa, S. Verosky, A. Luerssen, and O. N. Ayduk. 2012. Individual differences in neural responses to social rejection: The joint effect of self-esteem and attentional control. *Social Cognitive and Affective Neuroscience* 7, 3: 322–31.

Haggard, P. 2017. Sense of agency in the human brain. *Nature Reviews Neuroscience* 18, 4: 196–207.

Hajo, A., O. Obodaru, and A. Galinsky. 2015. Who you are is where you are: Antecedents and consequences of locating the self in the brain or the heart. *Organizational Behavior and Human Decision Processes* 128: 74–83.

Hameroff, S. 2001. Consciousness, the brain, and spacetime geometry. *Annals of the New York Academy of Sciences* 929 (April): 74–104.

Hanfstingl, B. 2013. Ego and spiritual transcendence: Relevance to psychological resilience and the role of age. *Evidence-Based Complementary and Alternative Medicine* 2013: 1–9. doi:10.1155/2013/949838.

Hardy, T. K., O. Govorun, R. H. Fazio, and R. M. Arkin. 2010 (May). Intellectual self-doubt is unrelated to level of intellect but related to accessibility of intelligence domain. Poster presented at the 22nd annual meeting of the Association for Psychological Science, Boston, MA.

Harker, L., and D. Keltner. 2001. Expressions of positive emotion in women's college yearbook pictures and their relationship to personality and life outcomes across adulthood. *Journal of Personality and Social Psychology* 80, 1: 112–24.

Hartung, F., P. Hagoort, and R. M. Willems. 2017. Readers select a comprehension mode independent of pronoun: Evidence from fMRI during narrative comprehension. *Brain and Language* 170 (July): 29–38.

Hassan, M., A. B. Nadeem, and A. Akhter. 2016. Impact of workplace spirituality on job satisfaction: Mediating effect of trust. *Cogent Business and Management* 3, 1: n.p. doi:org/10.1080/23311975.2016.1189808.

Hauggard, P., C. M. Stancu, P. B. Brockoff, I. Thorsdottir, and L. Lahteenmaki. 2016. Determinants of meal satisfaction in a workplace environment. *Appetite* 1, 105: 195–203.

Hayes, S. C., J. B. Luoma, F. W. Bond, A. Masuda, and J. Lillis. 2006. Acceptance and commitment therapy: Model, processes, and outcomes. *Behaviour Research and Therapy* 44, 1: 1–25.

Hellstrom, C. 2001. Temporal dimensions of the self-concept: Entrapped and possible selves in chronic pain. *Psychology and Health* 16, 1: 111–24.

Henningsen, D. D., and M. L. M. Henningsen. 2017. Nuanced aggression in group decision making. *International Journal of Business Communication* 52: 188–204.

Heshmat, S. 2015. The scarcity mindset. Science of choice. *Psychology Today* (blog). Posted April 2, 2015. https://www.psychologytoday.com/us/blog/science -choice/201504/the-scarcity-mindset.

Hoefler, A., U. Athenstaedt, K. Corcoran, F. Ebner, and A. Ischebeck. 2015. Coping with self-threat and the evaluation of self-related traits: An fMRI study. *PLoS ONE* 10, 9. e0136027.

Holder, M. D., B. Coleman, and J. M. Wallace. 2008. Spirituality, religiousness, and happiness in children aged 8–12 years. *Journal of Happiness Studies* 11, 2: 131–150. doi:10.1007/s10902-008-9126-1.

Hood, B., S. Weltzien, L. Marsh, and P. Kanngiesser. 2016. Picture yourself: Self-focus and the endowment effect in preschool children. *Cognition* 152 (July): 70–77.

Hood, R. W. 2002. The mystical self: Lost and found. *International Journal for the Psychology of Religion* 12, 1: 1–14.

Horita, R. 2013. The influence of meaning making following stressful life experiences on change of self-concept. *Japanese Journal of Psychology* 84, 4: 408–18.

Howe, L. C., and Dweck, C. S. 2015. Changes in self-definition impede recovery from rejection. *Personality and Social Psychology Bulletin* 42, 1: 54–71.

Huebner, B. 2014. *Macrocognition: A Theory of Distributed Minds and Collective Intentionality.* New York: Oxford University Press.

Hung, L., and R. A. Bryant. 2016. Autobiographical memory in the angry self. *PLoS ONE* 11, 3: e0151349. doi:10.1371/journal.pone.0151349.

Hurlemann, R., and N. Marsh. 2016. New insights into the neuroscience of human altruism. *Nervenartz* 87, 11: 1131–35.

Ian, N. J., and J. Larsen. 2011. Wanting more than you have and its consequences for well-being. *Journal of Happiness Studies* 12, 5: 877–85.

IIM: International Institute of Management. 2005. Happiness economics: Gross National Happiness and Wellness Index. *IIM, Economics Journal Working Papers* 1, 1: n.p.

JadidMilani, M., T. Ashktorab, Z. AbedSaeedi, and H. AlaviMajd. 2015. The impact of self-transcendence on physical health status promotion in multiple sclerosis patients attending peer support groups. *International Journal of Nursing Practice* 21, 6: 725–32.

James, W. 1892. *Principles of Psychology*. New York: Henry Holt and Company.

Jose, P. E., B. T. Lim, and F. B. Byrant. 2012. Does savoring increase happiness? A daily diary study. *Journal of Positive Psychology* 7, 3: 176–87.

Josipovic, Z. 2013. Neural correlates of nondual awareness in meditation. *Annals of the New York Academy of Sciences* 1307 (January): 9–18. doi:10.1111/nyas.12261.

Jung, C. 1997. *Jung on Active Imagination*. Edited by J. Chodorow. Princeton, NJ. Princeton University Press.

Kahneman, D. 2011. *Thinking Fast and Slow*. New York: Farrar, Straus and Giroux.

Kan, C., M. Karasawa, and S. Kitayama. 2009. Minimalist in style: Self, identity, and well-being in Japan. *Self and Identity* 8, 2–3: 300–317.

Kaplan, A., and J. K. Garner. 2017. A complex dynamic systems perspective on identity and its development: The dynamic systems model of role identity. *Developmental Psychology* 53, 11: 2036–51.

Kapser, C., M. Vierbuchen, U. Ernst, S. Fischer, R. Radersma, A. Raulo, F. Cunha-Saraiva, M. Wu, K. B. Mobley, and B. Taborsky. 2017. Genetics and developmental biology of cooperation. *Molecular Ecology* 26, 17: 4364–77.

Kashdan, T. B. 2010. Psychological flexibility as a fundamental aspect of health. *Clinical Psychology Review* 30, 7: 865–78.

Kashdan, T. B., J. D. Elhai, and B. C. Frueh. 2006. Anhedonia and emotional numbing in combat veterans with PTSD. *Behaviour Research and Therapy* 44, 3: 457–67.

Kasser T., K. L. Rosenblum, A. J. Sameroff, E. L. Deci, C. P. Niemiec, R. M. Ryan, O. Arnadottir, R. Bond, H. Dittmar, N. Dungan, and S. Hawks. 2014. Changes in materialism, changes in psychological well-being: Evidence from three longitudinal studies and an intervention experiment. *Motivation and Emotion* 38, 1: 1–22.

Kasser T., and K. Sheldon. 2009. Time affluence as a path toward personal happiness and ethical business practice: Empirical evidence from four studies. *Journal of Business Ethics* 84, supplement 2: 243–55.

Kauffman, K. P. 2015. Emotional sentience and the nature of phenomenal experience. *Integral Biomathics: Life Sciences, Mathematics, and Phenomenological Philosophy, Progress in Biophysics and Molecular Biology* 119, 3: 545–62.

Kerr, C. E., M. D. Sacchet, S. W. Lazar, C. I. Moore, and S. R. Jones. 2013. Mindfulness starts with the body: Somatosensory attention and top-down modulation of cortical alpha rhythms in mindfulness meditation. *Frontiers in Human Neuroscience* 13, 7: 12.

Kervyn, N., S. T. Fiske, and V. Y. Yzerbyt. 2013. Integrating the stereotype content model (warmth and competence) and the Osgood semantic differential (evaluation, potency, and activity). *European Journal of Social Psychology* 43, 7: 673–81.

Keyes, Corey L. M. 2000. Subjective change and mental health: A self-concept theory. *Social Psychology Quarterly* 63, 3: 264–79.

Khanna, S., and B. Greyson. 2015. Near-death experiences and post-traumatic growth. *Journal of Nervous and Mental Disease* 203, 10: 749–55.

Kim, J. H., Y. D. Son, J. H. Kim, E. J. Choi, S. Y. Lee, Y. H. Joo, Y. B. Kim, and Z. H. Cho. 2015. Research report: Self-transcendence trait and its relationship with in vivo serotonin transporter availability in brainstem raphe nuclei: An ultrahigh resolution PET-MRI study. *Brain Research* 10, 1629: 63–71.

Kim, S. H., L. C. Vincent, and J. H. Goncalo. 2013. Outside advantage: Can social rejection fuel creative thought? *Journal of Experimental Psychology: General* 142, 3: 605–11.

King, U. 2011. Can spirituality transform our world? *Journal for the Study of Spirituality* 1, 1: 17–34.

Klein, S. B. 2012. Self, memory, and the self-reference effect: An examination of conceptual and methodological issues. *Personality and Social Psychology Review* 16, 3: 283–300.

Kline, M., P. A. Cowan, and C. P. Cowan. 1991. The origins of parental stress during the transition to parenthood: A new family model. *Early Education and Development* 2, 4: 287–305.

Koenig, H. G. 2012. Religion, spirituality, and health: The research and clinical implications. *International Scholarly Research Notes* 16 (December): 278730. doi:10.5402/2012/278730.

Koerner, E. F. 1992. The Sapir-Whorf hypothesis: A preliminary history and a bibliographical essay. *Journal of Linguistic Anthropology* 2, 2: 173–98.

Konopka, L. M. 2015. Near death experience: Neuroscience perspective. *Croatian Medical Journal* 56, 4: 392–93.

Koriat, A. 2012. Confidence in personal preferences. *Journal of Behavioral Decision Making* 26, 3: 247–259.

Kraus, M. W., S. Cote, and D. Keltner. 2010. Social class, contextualism, and empathic accuracy. *Psychological Science* 21, 11: 1716–23.

Kross, E. 2009. When the self becomes other. *Annals of the New York Academy of Sciences* 1167: 35–40.

Kross, E., M. G. Berman, W. Mischel, E. E. Smith, and T. D. Wager. 2011. Social rejection shares somatosensory representations with physical pain. *Proceedings of the National Academy of Sciences of the United States of America* 108, 15: 6270–75.

Kross, E., E. Bruehlman-Senecal, J. Park, A. Burson, A. Dougherty, H. Shablack, R. Bremner, J. Moser, and O. Ayduk. 2014. Self-talk as a regulatory mechanism: How you do it matters. *Journal of Personality and Social Psychology* 106, 2: 304–24.

Kross, E., T. Egner, K. Ochsner, J. Hirsch, and G. Downey. 2007. Neural dynamics of rejection sensitivity. *Journal of Cognitive Neuroscience* 19, 6: 945–56.

Kusner, K. G., Mahoney, A., K. I. Pargament, and A. DeMaris. 2014. Sanctification of marriage and spiritual intimacy predicting observed marital interactions across the transition to parenthood. *Journal of Family Psychology* 28, 5: 604–14.

Lafreniere, M. K., R. J. Vallerand, and C. Sedikides. 2013. On the relation between self-enhancement and life satisfaction: The moderating role of passion. *Self and Identity* 12, 6: 597–609.

Laham, S. M., P. Koval, and A. Alter. 2012. The name-pronunciation effect: Why people like Mr. Smith more than Mr. Colquhoun. *Journal of Experimental Social Psychology* 48: 752–56.

Lahvis, G. P. 2017. Social reward and empathy as proximal contributions to altruism: The camaraderie effect. *Current Topics in Behavioral Neurosciences* 30: 127–57.

Laird, M. D., P. Harvey, and J. Lancaster. 2015. Accountability, entitlement, tenure, and job satisfaction in Generation Y. *Journal of Managerial Psychology* 30, 1: 87–100.

Lakey, C. E., J. K. Hirsch, L. A. Nelson, and S. A. Nsamenang. 2014. Effects of contingent self-esteem on depressive symptoms and suicidal behavior. *Death Studies* 38, 9: 563–70.

Lang, S. 2014. *Toki Pona: The Language of Good*. Tawhid: No place of publication given.

Latzman, R. D., and A. Masuda. 2013. Examining mindfulness and psychological inflexibility within the framework of Big Five personality. *Personality and Individual Differences* 55: 129–34.

Layous, K., J. Kurtz, J. Chancellor, and S. Lyubomirsky. 2017. Reframing the ordinary: Imagining time as scarce increases well-being. *Journal of Positive Psychology* 13, 3: 1–8. doi:10.1080/17439760.2017.1279210.

Le, T. N., and M. R. Levenson. 2005. Wisdom as self-transcendence: What's love (and individualism) got to do with it? *Journal of Research in Personality* 39, 4: 443–57.

Leach, C. W., N. Ellemers, and M. Barreto. 2007. Group virtue: The importance of morality (vs. competence and sociability) on the positive evaluation of in-groups. *Journal of Personality and Social Psychology* 93, 2: 234–49.

Lee, Y. H., Y. J. Shiah, S. C. Chen, S. F. Wang, M. S. Young, and C. L. Lin. 2015. Improved emotional stability in experienced meditators with concentrative meditation based on electroencephalography and heart rate variability. *Journal of Alternative and Complementary Medicine* 21, 1: 31–39.

Leitner, J. B., E. Hehman, M. P. Deegan, and J. M. Jones. 2014. Adaptive disengagement buffers self-esteem from negative social feedback. *Personality and Social Psychology Bulletin* 40, 11: 1435–50.

Levenson, M. R., P. A. Jennings, C. M. Aldwin, and R. W. Shiraishi. 2005. Self-transcendence: Conceptualization and measurement. *International Journal of Aging and Human Development* 60, 2: 127–43.

Levin, M. E., J. B. Luoma, R. Vilardaga, J. Lillis, R. Nobles, and S. C. Hayes. 2016. Examining the role of psychological inflexibility, perspective taking, and empathic concern in generalized prejudice. *Journal of Applied Social Psychology* 46, 3: 180–91.

Li, C. S., and R. Sinha. 2008. Inhibitory control and emotional stress regulation: Neuroimaging evidence for frontal-limbic dysfunction in psycho-stimulant addiction. *Neuroscience and Biobehavioral Reviews* 32, 3: 581–97.

Lindebaum, D., and D. Geddes. 2015. The place and role of (moral) anger in organizational behavior studies. *Journal of Organizational Behavior* 37, 5: 738–57.

Lisbet, B., C. A. Gleason, E. W. Wright, and D. K. Pearl. 1983. Time of conscious intention to act in relation to onset of cerebral activity (readiness-potential): The unconscious initiation of a freely voluntary act. *Brain* 106, 3: 623–42.

Liu, P., F. Zhao, B. Zhang, and Q. Dang. 2017. Small change makes a big splash: The role of working self-concept in the effects of stereotype threat on memory. *Journal of Psychology* 151, 7: 613–31.

Liu, X., Z. Shi, Y. Ma, J. Qin, and S. Han. 2013. Dynamic neural processing of linguistic cues related to death. *PLoS ONE* 8, 6: e67905.

Loevinger, J. 1976. *Ego Development.* San Francisco: Jossey-Bass.

Lu, L., J. D. Shepard, F. S. Hall, and Y. Shaham. 2003. Effect of environmental stressors on opiate and psychostimulant reinforcement, reinstatement, and discrimination in rats: A review. *Neuroscience and Biobehavioral Reviews* 27, 5: 457–91.

Lyons, D. M., and K. J. Parker. 2007. Stress inoculation–induced indications of resilience in monkeys. *Journal of Traumatic Stress* 20, 4: 423–33.

Mackinnon, S. P. 2015. Multidimensional self-esteem and test derogation after negative feedback. *Canadian Journal of Behavioural Science* 47, 1: 123–26.

Macrae, C. N., J. M. Moran, T. F. Heatherton, J. F. Banfield, and W. M. Kelley. 2004. Medial prefrontal activity predicts memory for self. *Cerebral Cortex* 14, 6: 647–54.

Majdandzic, J., S. Amashaufer, A. Hummer, C. Windischberger, and C. Lamm. 2016. The selfless mind: How prefrontal involvement in mentalizing with similar and dissimilar others shapes empathy and prosocial behavior. *Cognition* 157: 24–38.

Mandel, N. A., D. D. Rucker, J. C. Levav, and A. D. Galinsky. 2014. Research review—The compensatory consumer behavior model: How self-discrepancies drive consumer behavior. *Journal of Consumer Psychology* 27, 1: 133–46.

Mani, A., S. Mullainathan, E. Shafir, and J. Zhao. 2013. Poverty impedes cognitive function. *Science* 341, 6149: 976–80.

Marraffa, M. 2013. DeMartino, Jervis, and the self-defensive nature of self-consciousness. *Paradigmi* 31, 2: 109–24.

Marraffa, M., and A. Paternoster. 2016. Disentangling the self: A naturalistic approach to narrative self-construction. *New Ideas in Psychology* 40: 115–22.

Maslow, A. H. 1943. A theory of human motivation. *Psychological Review 50, 4*: 370–96.

———. 1970a. *Motivation and Personality.* New York: Harper & Row.

———. 1970b. *Religions, Values, and Peak Experiences.* New York: Penguin. (Original work published 1964.)

Masuda, A., and E. C. Tully. 2011. The role of mindfulness and psychological flexibility in somatization, depression, anxiety, and general psychological distress in a nonclinical college sample. *Journal of Evidence-Based Complementary and Alternative Medicine* 17, 1: 66–71.

Mathur, V. A., B. K. Cheon, T. Harada, J. Scimeca, and J. Y. Chiao. 2016. Overlapping neural response to the pain or harm of people, animals, and nature. *Neuropsychologia* 81: 265–73.

Mattingly, B. A., and G. W. Lewandowski. 2013. An expanded self is a more capable self: The association between self-concept size and self-efficacy. *Self and Identity* 12, 6: 621–34.

Max-Neef, M. A., A. Elizalde, and M. Hopenhayn. 1989. Development and human needs. In M. A. Max-Neef (ed.), *Human Scale Development: Conception, Application, and Further Reflections,* 13–47. New York: Apex.

McAdams, D. P., E. D. St. Aubin, and R. L. Logan. 1993. Generativity among young, midlife, and older adults. *Psychology and Aging* 8, 2: 221–30.

McCarthy, V. L., L. Jiying, and R. M. Carini. 2013. The role of self-transcendence. *Research in Gerontological Nursing* 6, 3: 178–86.

McClintock, C. H., E. Lau, and L. Miller. 2016. Phenotypic dimensions of spirituality: Implications for mental health in China, India, and the United States. *Frontiers in Psychology* 7: 1600.

McIntyre, M. 2016. Overcome the imposter syndrome. *Communication Briefings* 35, 2: 8.

McKechnie, C. C. 2014. Anxieties of communication: The limits of narrative in the medical humanities. *Medical Humanities* 40, 2: 119–24.

McLeod, B. D., J. R. Weisz, and J. J. Wood. 2007a. Examining the relationship between parenting and childhood depression: A meta-analysis. *Clinical Psychology Review* 27, 8: 986–1003.

McLeod, B. D., J. J. Wood, and J. R. Weisz. 2007b. Examining the association between parenting and childhood anxiety: A meta-analysis. *Clinical Psychology Review* 27, 2: 155–72.

McPherson, M., L. Smith-Lovin, and M. E. Brashears. 2006. Social isolation in America: Changes in core discussion networks over two decades. *American Sociological Review* 71, 3: 353–75.

Melucci, A. 1995. *The Process of Collective Identity*. Philadelphia: Temple University Press.

Merolla, D. M., R. T. Serpe, S. Stryker, and P. W. Schultz. 2012. Structural precursors to identity processes. *Social Psychology Quarterly* 75, 2: 149–72.

Metz, T. 2014. Gross national happiness: A philosophical appraisal. *Ethics and Social Welfare* 8, 3: 218–32.

Midgley, G. 1994. Ecology and the poverty of humanism: A critical systems perspective. *Systems Research and Behavioral Science* 11, 4: 67–76.

Miller, J. D., J. L. Maples, L. Buffardi, H. Cai, B. Gentile, Y. Kisbu-Sakarya, V. S. Kwan, A. LoPilato, L. F. Pendry, C. Sedikides, L. Siedor, and W. K. Campbell. 2015. Narcissism and United States' culture: The view from home and around the world. *Journal of Personality and Social Psychology* 109, 6: 1068–89.

Mills, P. J., C. T. Peterson, M. A. Pung, S. Patel, L. Weiss, K. L. Wilson, M. Doraiswarmy, J. A. Martin, R. E. Tanzi, and D. Chopra. 2017. Change in sense of nondual awareness and spiritual awakening in response to a multidimensional well-being program. *Journal of Alternative and Complementary Medicine* 00, 00: 1–9.

Mirams, L., E. Poliakoff, R. J. Brown, and D. M. Lloyd. 2013. Brief body-scan meditation practice improves somatosensory perceptual decision making. *Conscious Cognition* 22, 1: 348–59.

Mirels, L. H., P. Greblo, and J. B. Dean. 2002. Judgmental self-doubt: Beliefs about one's judgmental prowess. *Personality and Individual Differences* 33: 741–58.

Mirucka, B., U. Bielecka, and M. Kisielewska. 2016. Positive orientation, self-esteem, and satisfaction with life in the context of subjective age in older adults. *Personality and Individual Differences* 99: 209–10.

Mischkowski, D., E. Kross, and B. J. Bushman. 2012. Flies on the wall are less aggressive: Self-distancing "in the heat of the moment" reduces aggressive thoughts, angry feelings, and aggressive behavior. *Journal of Experimental Social Psychology* 48, 5: 1187–91.

Mogilner, C., Z. Chance, and M. I. Norton. 2012. Giving time gives you time. *Psychological Science* 23, 10: 1233–38.

Monceri, F. 2009. The transculturing self, part II. Constructing identity through identification. *Language and Intercultural Communication* 9, 1: 43–53.

Montecucco, N. F. 2006. Coherence, brain evolution, and the unity of consciousness: The evolution of planetary consciousness in light of brain coherence research. *World Futures: The Journal of New Paradigm Research* 62, 1–2: 127–33.

———. 2016. The consciousness (r)evolution paradigm. *World Futures: The Journal of New Paradigm Research* 72, 3–4: 167–86.

Moore, J. W. 2016. What is the sense of agency and why does it matter? *Frontiers in Psychology* 7: 1272.

Moore, J. W., and P. C. Fletcher. 2012. Sense of agency in health and disease: A review of cue integration approaches. *Consciousness and Cognition* 21, 1: 59–68.

Mor, N., and J. Winquist. 2002. Self-focused attention and negative affect: A meta-analysis. *Psychological Bulletin* 128, 4: 638–62.

Morris, R. C. 2013. Identity salience and identity importance in identity theory. *Current Research in Social Psychology* 21, 8: 23–36.

Mullainathan, S., and E. Shafir. 2013. *Scarcity: Why Having Too Little Means So Much*. New York: Time Books/Henry Holt and Company.

Murray, S. L., J. G. Holmes, D. W. Griffin, G. Bellavia, and P. Rose. 2001. The mismeasure of love: How self-doubt contaminates relationship beliefs. *Personality and Social Psychology Bulletin* 27, 4: 423–36.

Murray, S. L., J. G. Holmes, G. MacDonald, and P. C. Ellsworth. 1998. Through the looking glass darkly? When self-doubts turn into relationship insecurities. *Journal of Personality and Social Psychology* 75, 6: 1459–80.

Na, J., and L. Choi. 2009. Culture and first-person pronouns. *Personality and Social Psychology Bulletin* 35, 11: 1492–99.

Napier, A. D. 2012. Nonself help: How immunology might reframe the enlightenment. *Cultural Anthropology: Journal of the Society for Cultural Anthropology* 27, 1: 122–37.

Neff, K. 2011. *Self-Compassion.* New York: HarperCollins Publishers.

Niemiec, C., K. W. Brown, T. B. Kashdan, P. J. Cozzolini, W. E. Breen, C. Levesque-Bristol, and R. M. Ryan. 2010. Being present in the face of existential threat: The role of trait mindfulness in reducing defensive responses to mortality salience. *Journal of Personality and Social Psychology* 99, 2: 344–65.

Nisbett, R. E. 2003. *The Geography of Thought: How Asians and Westerners Think Differently...and Why.* New York: Free Press.

Nix, R. L., E. E. Pinderhughes, K. A. Dodge, J. E. Bates, G. S. Pettite, and S. A. McFayden-Ketchum. 1999. The relation between mothers' hostile attribution tendencies and children's externalizing behavior problems: The mediating role of mothers' harsh discipline practices. *Child Development* 70, 4: 896–909.

Northoff, G., P. Qin, and T. E. Feinberg. 2011. Brain imaging of the self: Conceptual, methodological, and empirical issues. *Consciousness and Cognition* 20, 1: 52–63.

Northoff, G., A. Heinzel, M. de Greck, F. Bermpohl, H. Dobrowolny, and J. Panksepp. 2006. Self-referential processing on our brain: A meta-analysis of imaging studies on the self. *NeuroImage* 31, 1: 440–57.

Novotney, A. 2014. The psychology of scarcity. *Monitor on Psychology* 45, 2: 28.

O'Brien, D. T. 2014. An evolutionary model of the environmental conditions that shape the development of prosociality. *Evolutionary Psychology* 12, 2: 386–402.

Oh, D. S., and J. D. Choi. 2017. The effect of motor imagery training for trunk movements on trunk muscle control and proprioception in stroke patients. *Journal of Physical Therapy Science* 29, 7: 1224–28

Oleson, K. C., K. M. Poehlmann, J. H. Yost, M. E. Lynch, and R. M. Arkin. 2000. Subjective overachievement: Individual differences in self-doubt and concern with performance. *Journal of Personality* 68, 3: 491–524.

Orth, U., K. H. Trzesniewski, and R. W. Robins. 2010. Self-esteem development from young adulthood to old age: A cohort-sequential longitudinal study. *Journal of Personality and Social Psychology* 98, 4: 645–58.

Ortigue, S., and F. Bianchi-Demicheli. 2008. Why is your spouse so predictable? Connecting mirror neuron system and self-expansion model of love. *Medical Hypotheses* 71, 6: 941–44.

Ochsner, K. N., K. Knierim, D. H. Ludlow, J. Hanelin, T. Ramachandran, and G. Glover. 2004. Reflection upon feelings: An fMRI study of neural systems supporting the attribution of emotion to self and other. *Journal of Cognitive Neuroscience* 16, 10: 1746–72.

Ostafin, B. D., G. A. Mariatt, and W. Troop-Gordon. 2010. Testing the incentive-sensitization theory with at-risk drinkers: Wanting, liking, and alcohol consumption. *Psychology of Addictive Behaviors* 24, 1: 157–62.

Overwalle, F. V. 2008. Social cognition and the brain: A meta-analysis. *Human Brain Mapping* 30, 3: 829–58.

Pally, S. 1955. Cognitive rigidity as a function of threat. *Journal of Personality* 23, 3: 346.

Panaioti, A. 2015. Mindfulness and personal identity in the Western cultural context: A plea for greater cosmopolitanism. *Transcultural Psychiatry* 52, 4: 501–23.

Panksepp, J. 2005. On the embodied emotional neural nature of core emotional affects. *Journal of Consciousness Studies* 12, 8–10: 158–84.

Parent, J., L. G. McKee, J. N. Rough, and R. Forehand. 2016. The association of parent mindfulness with parenting and youth psychopathology across three developmental stages. *Journal of Abnormal Child Psychology* 44, 1: 191–202.

Park, J. K., and D. R. John. 2011. More than meets the eye: The influence of implicit and explicit self-esteem on materialism. *Journal of Consumer Psychology* 21: 73–87.

Park, K., and C. Chung. 2016. Establishing a fear extinction–impaired animal model of post-traumatic stress disorder. *International Journal of Neuropsychopharmacology* 19, 1: 92.

Parnell, L. 2013. *Attachment-Focused EMDR: Healing Relational Trauma.* New York: W. W. Norton.

Penny, D. 2014. Cooperation and selfishness both occur during molecular evolution. *Biology Direct* 10, 1: 1–16.

Pepping, C. A., A. O'Donovan, and P. J. Davis. 2013. The positive effects of mindfulness on self-esteem. *Journal of Positive Psychology* 8, 5: 376–86.

Perach, R., and A. Wisman. 2016. Can creativity beat death? A review and evidence on the existential anxiety buffering functions of creative achievement. *Journal of Creative Behavior.* doi:10.1002/jocb.171.

Peters, J. R., T. A. Eisenlohr-Moul, and L. M. Smart. 2016. Dispositional mindfulness and rejection sensitivity: The critical role of nonjudgment. *Personality and Individual Differences* 93: 125–29.

Piff, P. K., M. W. Kraus, S. Cote, B. H. Cheng, and D. Keltner. 2010. Having less, giving more: The influence of social class on prosocial behavior. *Journal of Personality and Social Psychology* 99, 5: 771–84.

Piff, P. K., D. M. Stancato, S. Cote, R. Mendoza-Denton, and D. Keltner. 2012. Higher class predicts increased unethical behavior. *Proceedings of the National Academy of Sciences* 109, 11: 4086–91.

Pilarska, A. 2014. Self-construal as a mediator between identity structure and subjective well-being. *Current Psychology* 33, 2: 130–54.

Pittman, T. S., and K. R. Zeigler. 2007. Basic human needs. In A. Kruglanski and E. T. Higgins (eds.), *Social Psychology: Handbook of Basic Principles*, 2nd ed., 473–89. New York: Guilford.

Plant, D. T., F. W. Jones, C. M. Pariante, and S. Pawlby. 2017. Association between maternal childhood trauma and offspring childhood psychopathology: Mediation analysis from the ALSPAC cohort. *British Journal of Psychiatry* 211, 3: 144–50.

Plotkin, B. 2008. *Nature and the Human Soul: Cultivating Wholeness and Community in a Fragmented World*. Novato, CA: New World Library.

Porter, M. E., and S. Stern. 2017. Social Progress Index 2017. *Social Progress Imperative 2017*. https://www.socialprogressindex.com/.

Prabhu, H. R., and P. S. Bhat. 2013. Mind and consciousness in yoga—Vedanta: A comparative analysis with Western psychological concepts. *Indian Journal of Psychiatry* 55, supplement 2: 182–86.

Priesemuth, M., and R. Taylor. 2016. The more I want, the less I have to give: The moderating role of psychological entitlement on the relationship between psychological contract violation, depressive mood states, and citizenship behavior. *Journal of Organizational Behavior* 37, 7: 967–82.

Pronin, E., and E. Jacobs. 2008. Thought speed, mood, and the experience of mental motion. *Perspectives on Psychological Science* 3, 6: 461–85.

Pronin, E., E. Jacobs, and D. M. Wegner. 2008. Psychological effects of thought acceleration. *Emotion* 8, 5: 597–612.

Pyszczynski, T., J. Greenberg, S. Solomon, J. Arndt, and J. Schimel. 2004. Why do people need self-esteem? A theoretical and empirical review. *Psychology Bulletin* 130, 3: 435–68.

Rabinovich, A., and T. A. Morton. 2016. Coping with identity conflict: Perceptions of self as flexible vs. fixed moderate the effect of identity conflict on well-being. *Self and Identity* 15, 2: 224–44.

Rand, D. G., and Z. G. Epstein. 2014. Risking your life without a second thought: Intuitive decision making and extreme altruism. *PLoS ONE*, 9, 10: e109687.

Rand, D. G., J. D. Greene, and M. A. Nowak. 2012. Spontaneous giving and calculated greed. *Nature: International Weekly Journal of Science* 489: 427–30.

Ranganathan, V. K., V. Siemionow, J. Z. Liu, V. Sahgal, and G. H. Yue. 2004. From mental power to muscle power: Gaining strength by using the mind. *Neuropsychologia* 42, 7: 944–56.

Raskin, R., and R. Shaw. 1988. Narcissism and the use of personal pronouns. *Journal of Personality* 56, 2: 393–404.

Reich-Graefe, R. 2014. Calculative trust: Oxymoron or tautology? *Journal of Trust Research* 4, 1: 66–82.

Reimer, H., H. R. Markus, S. Shavitt, and M. Koo. 2014. Preferences don't have to be personal: Expanding attitude theorizing with a cross-cultural perspective. *Psychological Review* 121, 4: 619–48.

Ritchie, T. D., C. Sedikides, T. Wildschut, J. Arndt, and Y. Gidron. 2011. Self-concept clarity mediates the relation between stress and subjective well-being. *Self and Identity* 10, 4: 493–508.

Robins, R. W., K. H. Trzesniewski, J. L. Tracy, S. D. Gosling, and J. Potter. 2002. Global self-esteem across the lifespan. *Psychology and Aging* 17, 3: 423–34.

Robinson, M. R., A. Kleinman, G. Mariaelisa, A. A. E. Vinkhuyzen, D. Couper, M. B. Miller, W. J. Peyrot, A. Abdellaoui, B. P. Zietsch, I. M. Nolte, J. Van Vliet-Ostaptchouk, and H. Sneider. 2017. Genetic evidence of assertive mating in humans. *Nature, Human Behavior* 1, 1. doi:10.1038/s41562-016-0016.

Robison, M. 2014. Are people naturally inclined to cooperate or be selfish? *Scientific American Mind: Behavior and Society* online; Sept 1.

Rochat, P. 2003. Five levels of self-awareness as they unfold early in life. *Consciousness and Cognition* 12, 4: 717–31.

———. 2001. *The Infant's World.* Cambridge, MA: Harvard University Press.

Rogers, T. W., and A. Friedberg. 2016. A conjecture on the nature and evolution of consciousness. *Neuropsychoanalysis: An Interdisciplinary Journal for Psychoanalysis and the Neurosciences* 18, 2: 147–61.

Rosch, E. H. 1973. Natural categories. *Cognitive Psychology* 4, 3: 328–50.

Rose, J., N. Roman, K. Mwaba, and K. Ismail. 2017. The relationship between parenting and internalizing behavior of children: A systematic review. *Early Child Development and Care* 12 (January): 1–19.

Roux, C., K. Goldsmith, and A. Bonezzi. 2015. On the psychology of scarcity: When reminders of resource scarcity promote selfish (and generous) behavior. *Journal of Consumer Research* 42, 4: 615–31.

Rudan, D., M. Jakovljevic, and D. Marcinko. 2016. Manic defenses in contemporary society: The psychocultural approach. *Psychiatria Danubina* 28, 4: 334–42.

Ruedy, N., and M. Schweitzer. 2010. In the moment: The effect of mindfulness on ethical decision making. *Journal of Business Ethics* 95, 1: 73–87.

Rueppell O., M. K. Hayworth, and N. P. Ross. 2010. Altruistic self-removal of health-compromised honey bee workers from their hives. *Journal of Evolutionary Biology* 23, 7: 1538–46.

Runquist, J. J., and P. G. Reed. 2007. Self-transcendence and well-being in homeless adults. *Journal of Holistic Nursing* 25, 1: 5–13.

Russac, R. J. 2007. Death anxiety across the adult years: An examination of age and gender effects. *Death Studies* 31, 6: 549–61.

Ryan, R. M., and E. L. Deci. 2002. Self-determination theory and the facilitation of intrinsic motivation, social development, and well-being. *American Psychologist* 55, 1: 68–78.

Saad, M., R. de Medeiros, and A. C. Mosini. 2017. Are we ready for a true biopsychosocial-spiritual model? The many meanings of "spiritual." *Medicines* (Basel, Switzerland) 4, 4: 79. doi:10.3390/medicines4040079.

Sabey, A. K., A. J. Rauer, and J. F. Jensen. 2014. Compassionate love as a mechanism linking sacred qualities of marriage to older couples' marital satisfaction. *Journal of Family Psychology* 28, 5: 594–603.

Sairanen, E., A. Tolvanin, L. Karhunen, M. Kolehmanien, E. Jarvela, S. Rantala, K. Peuhkuri, R. Korpela, and R. Lappalainen. 2015. Psychological flexibility and mindfulness explain intuitive eating in overweight adults. *Behavior Modification* 39, 4: 557–79.

Sakulku, J. 2011. The imposter phenomenon. *International Journal of Behavioral Science* 6, 1: 73–92.

Sansone, R. A., and L. A. Sansone. 2010. Road rage: What's driving it? *Psychiatry (Edgmont)* 7, 7: 14–18.

Schachtel, H. 1954. *The Real Enjoyment of Living.* New York: Dutton.

Scheier, M. F., C. S. Carver, and F. X. Gibbons. 1979. Self-directed attention, awareness of bodily states, and suggestibility. *Journal of Personality and Social Psychology* 37, 9: 1576–88.

Schneider, F., F. Bermpohl, A. Heinzel, M. Rotte, M. Walter, C. Tempelmann, C. Wiebking, H. Dobrowolny, H. J. Heinze, and G. Northoff. 2008. The resting brain and our self: Self-relatedness modulates resting state neural activity in cortical midline structures. *Neuroscience* 157, 1: 120–31.

Schoenberg, P. L. A., A. Ruf, J. Churchill, D. P. Brown, and J. A. Brewer. 2017. Mapping complex mind states: EED neural substrates of meditative unified compassionate awareness. *Consciousness and Cognition* 57: 41–53.

Schooler, C., M. S. Mulatu, and G. Oats. 1999. The continuing effects of substantively complex work on the intellectual functioning of older workers. *Psychology and Aging* 14, 3: 483–506.

Schuster, C., R. Hilfiker, O. Amft, A. Scheidhauer, B. Andrews, J. Butler, U. Kischka, and T. Ettlin. 2011. Best practice for motor imagery: A systematic literature review on motor imagery training elements in five different disciplines. *BMC Medicine* 9: 75. doi:10.1186/1741-7015-9-75/.

Schwarz, N. 2000. Social judgment and attitudes: Warmer, more social, and less conscious. *European Journal of Social Psychology* 30: 149–76.

Shallcross, A. J., A. S. Troy, M. Boland, and I. B. Maas. 2010. Let it be: Accepting negative emotional experiences predicts decreased negative affect and depressive symptoms. *Behaviour Research and Therapy* 48, 9: 921–29.

Shanta, B. A. 2015. Life and consciousness: The Vedāntic view. *Communicative and Integrative Biology* 8, 5: e1085138.

Sheldon, K. M., A. Wineland, L. Venhoeven, and E. Osin. 2016. *Ecopsychology* 8, 4: 228–38.

Shepperd, J. A., A. J. Rothman, and W. M. P. Klein. 2011. Using self- and identity-regulation to promote health: Promises and challenges. *Self and Identity* 10, 3: 407–16.

Sherif, M., and C. I. Hovland. 1980. *Social Judgment: Assimilation and Contrast Effects in Communication and Attitude Change*. Westport, CT: Greenwood.

Sherman, D. K., and G. L. Cohen. 2006. The psychology of self-defense: Self-affirmation theory. In M. P. Zanna (ed.), *Advances in Experimental Social Psychology, vol. 38*, 183–242. San Diego, CA: Academic.

Sherman, D. K., K. A. Hartson, K. R. Binning, V. Purdie-Vaughns, J. Garcia, S. Taborsky-Barba, S. Tomassetti, A. D. Nussbaum, and G. L. Cohen. 2013. Deflecting the trajectory and changing the narrative: How self-affirmation affects academic performance and motivation under identity threat. *Journal of Personality and Social Psychology* 104, 4: 591–618.

Shira, A., E. Bodner, and Y. Palgi. 2014. The interactive effect of subjective age and subjective distance-to-death on psychological distress of older adults. *Aging & Mental Health* 18, 8: 1066–70.

Shonin, E., W. Van Gordon, A. Compare, M. Zangeneh, and M. D. Griffiths. 2015. Buddhist-derived loving-kindness and compassion meditation for the treatment of psychopathology: A systematic review. *Mindfulness* 6, 5: 1161–80.

Shonin, E., W. Van Gordon, and M. D. Griffiths. 2013. Buddhist philosophy for the treatment of problem gambling. *Journal of Behavioral Addictions* 2, 2: 63–71.

Shultz, P. W., and A. Searleman. (2002). Rigidity of thought and behavior: One hundred years of research. *Genetic, Social, and General Psychology Monographs* 128, 2: 165–207.

Silvestre, G., and U. S. Landa. 2016. Women, physical activity, and quality of life: Self-concept as a mediator. *Spanish Journal of Psychology* 19 (February 22): E6. doi:10.1017/sjp.2016.4.

Sinha, R. 2008. Chronic stress, drug use, and vulnerability to addiction. *Annals of the New York Academy of Sciences.* 1141: 105–30.

Skowronski, J. J., and C. Sedikides. 2017. On the evolution of the human self: A data-driven review and reconsideration. *Self and Identity* (July): 1–18. doi:org /10.1080/15298868.2017.1350601.

Slingerland, E. 2015. Wu wei: Doing less and wanting more. *Psychologist* 28, 11: 882–85.

———. 2014. *Trying Not to Try: Ancient China, Modern Science, and the Power of Spontaneity.* New York: Crown Publishing.

Smilek, D., J. Enns, J. Eastwood, and P. Merikle. 2006. Relax! Cognitive strategy influences visual search. *Visual Cognition* 14, 4: 543–64.

Smith, L., K. Summers, and L. Harwell. 2012. A US Human Wellbeing Index (HWBI) for evaluating the influence of economic, social, and ecological service flow. Presented at Ecosystem Services Conference July 31–August 4, Portland, Oregon.

Snow, D., and C. Corrigall-Brown. "Collective Identity." In J. D. Wright (ed.), *International Encyclopedia of Social and Behavioral Sciences,* 2nd ed., 174–80. Oxford, UK: Elsevier.

Soenens, B. A., J. Elliot, L. Goosens, M. Vansteenkiste, P. Luyten, and B. Duirez. 2005. The intergenerational transmission of perfectionism: Parents' psychological control as an intervening variable. *Journal of Family Psychology* 19, 3: 358–66.

Sommer, K. L., and R. F. Baumeister. 2002. Self-evaluation, persistence, and performance following implicit rejection: The role of trait self-esteem. *Personality and Social Psychology Bulletin* 28, 7: 926–38.

Song, H., Z. Zou, K. Kou, Y. Liu, L. Yang, A. Zilverstand, F. Uquillas, and X. Zhang. 2015. Love-related changes in the brain: A resting-state functional magnetic resonance imaging study. *Frontiers in Human Neuroscience* 9 (February 13): 71. doi:10.3389/fnhum.2015.00071.

Spencer-Rogers, J., H. C. Boucher, S. C. Mori, W. Lei, and P. Kaiping. 2009. The dialectical self-concept: Contradiction, change, and holism in East Asian cultures. *Personality and Social Psychology Bulletin* 35, 1: 29–44.

Sperduti, M., P. Delaveau, F. Fossatti, and J. Nadel. 2011. Different brain structures related to self and external-agency attribution: A brief review and meta-analysis. *Brain Structure and Function* 216, 2: 151–57.

Stanley, M., and A. L. Burrow. 2015. The distance between selves: The influence of self-discrepancy on purpose in life. *Self and Identity* 14, 4: 441–52.

Stellar, J. E., V. M. Mazo, M. W. Kraus, and D. Keltner. 2012. Class and compassion: Socioeconomic factors predict responses to suffering. *Emotion* 12, 3: 449–59.

Stephens, A. N., and K. Ohtsuka. 2014. Cognitive biases in aggressive drivers. Does illusion of control drive us off the road? *Personality and Individual Differences* 68: 124–29.

Stewart, A. J., and J. B. Plotkin. 2013. Extortion and cooperation in the Prisoner's Dilemma. *Proceedings of the National Academy of Sciences* 109, 26: 10134–35.

Stone, H., and S. Stone. 1989. *Embracing Our Selves: The Voice Dialogue Manual.* Novato, CA: New World Library.

Subramanian, S. V., D. J. Kim, and I. Kawachi. 2002. Social trust and self-rated health in US communities: A multilevel analysis. *Journal of Urban Health: Bulletin of the New York Academy of Medicine* 79, supplement 1: S21–S34.

Sul, S., I. Choi, and P. Kang. 2012. Cultural modulation of self-referential brain activity for personality traits and social identities. *Social Neuroscience* 7, 3: 280–91.

Synofzik M., G. Vosgerau, and A. Newen. 2008. Beyond the comparator model: A multifactorial two-step account of agency. *Consciousness and Cognition* 17, 1: 219–39.

Szekeres, A., and R. Tisljar. 2013. Narcissism in the world of Facebook: An evolutionary psychopathological interpretation. *Psychiatria Hungrica* 28, 4: 440–53.

Tan, J., and C. Vogel. 2008. Religion and trust: An experimental study. *Journal of Economic Psychology* 9, 6: 832–48.

Tarrant, M. A., and H. K. Cordell. 2002. Amenity values of public and private forests: Examining the value-attitude relationship. *Environmental Management* 30, 5: 692–703.

Tassell-Matamua, N. A., and N. Lindsay. 2016. "I'm not afraid to die": The loss of the fear of death after a near-death experience. *Mortality* 21, 1: 71–87.

Tay, L., and E. Diener. 2011. Needs and subjective well-being around the world. *Journal of Personality and Social Psychology* 101, 2: 354.

Teasdale, J. D., R. G. Moore, H. Hayhurst, M. Pope, S. Williams, and Z. V. Segal. 2002. Metacognitive awareness and prevention of relapse in depression: Empirical evidence. *Journal of Consulting and Clinical Psychology* 70, 2: 275–87.

Tesser, A., M. Millar, and J. Moore. 1988. Some affective consequences of social comparison and reflection processes: The pain and pleasure of being close. *Journal of Personality and Social Psychology* 54, 1: 49–61.

Thoits, P. A. 1991. On merging identity theory and stress research. *Social Psychology Quarterly* 54, 2: 101–12.

———. 2012. Self, identity, stress, and mental health. In C. S. Aneshensel, J. C. Phelan, and A. Bierman (eds.), *Handbook of the Sociology of Mental Health*, 357–77. New York: Springer.

Thorgersen, J. H., J. Juhl, and C. S. Pulsen. 2009. Complaining: A function of attitude, personality, and situation. *Psychology and Marketing* 26, 8: 760–77.

Thorton, D., and A. J. Arrowood. 1966. Self-evaluation, self-enhancement, and the locus of social comparison. *Journal of Experimental Social Psychology*, supplement 1: 40–48.

Tomasino, B., A. Chiesa, and F. Frabbo. 2014. Disentangling the neural mechanisms involved in Hinduism- and Buddhism-related meditations. *Brain and Cognition* 90: 32–40.

Travis, F., A. Arenander, and D. DuBois. 2004. Psychological and physiological characteristics of a proposed object-referral/self-referral continuum of self-awareness. *Consciousness and Cognition* 13, 2: 401–20.

Travis, F., and J. Shear. 2010. Focused attention, open monitoring, and automatic self-transcending: Categories to organize meditations from Vedic, Buddhist, and Chinese traditions. *Consciousness and Cognition* 19, 4: 1110–18.

Trommsdorff, G. 2009. Culture and development of self-regulation. *Social and Personality Psychology Compass* 3, 5: 687–701.

Tsakiris, M., S. Schutz-Bosbach, and S. Gallagher. 2007. On agency and body ownership: Phenomenological and neurocognitive reflections. *Consciousness and Cognition* 16, 3: 645–60.

Turk, D. J., T. F. Heatherton, C. N. Macrae, W. M. Kelley, and M. S. Gazzaniga. 2003. Out of contact, out of mind: The distributed nature of the self. *Annals of the New York Academy of Sciences* 1001: 65–78.

Twenge, J. M., and J. D. Foster. 2010. Birth cohort increases in narcissistic personality traits among American college students, 1982–2009. *Social Psychological and Personality Science* 1, 1: 99–106.

Ulber, J., K. Hamann, and M. Tomasello. 2015. How 18- and 24-month-old peers divide resources among themselves. *Journal of Experimental Child Psychology* 140: 228–44.

Urgesi, C., S. Aglioti, M. Skrap, and F. Frabbo. 2010. Clinical study: The spiritual brain—Selective cortical lesions modulate human self-transcendence. *Neuron* 65, 3: 309–19.

Vago, D. R., and F. Zeidan. 2016. The brain on silent: Mind wandering, mindful awareness, and states of mental tranquility. *Annals of the New York Academy of Sciences* 1373, 1: 96–113.

Vaish, A., T. Grossmann, and A. Woodward. 2008. Not all emotions are created equal: The negativity bias in social-emotional development. *Psychological Bulletin* 134, 3: 383–403.

Vallverdu, J. 2017. Brains, language, and the argumentative mind in Western and Eastern societies: The fertile differences between Western-Eastern argumentative traditions. *Progress in Biophysics and Molecular Biology* 131: 424–31.

Van der Kolk, B. 2000. Post-traumatic stress disorder and the nature of trauma. *Dialogues in Clinical Neuroscience* 2, 1: 7–22.

Van Lange, P. A. 2008. Does empathy trigger only altruistic motivation? How about selflessness or justice? *Emotion* 8, 6: 766–74.

Verhagen, J. V. 2007. The neurocognitive bases of human multimodal food perception: Consciousness. *Brain Research Review* 53, 2: 271–86.

Vignoles, V. L., C. Regalia, C. Manzi, J. Golledge, and E. Scabini. 2006. Beyond self-esteem: Influence of multiple motives on identity construction. *Journal of Personality and Social Psychology* 90, 2: 308–33.

Vogeley, K., M. May, A. Ritzi, P. Falkai, K. Zilles, and G. R. Fink. 2004. Neural correlates of first-person perspective as one constituent of human self-consciousness. *Journal of Cognitive Neuroscience* 16, 5: 817–27.

Vohs, K. D., N. L. Mead, and M. R. Goode. 2006. The psychological consequences of money. *Science* 314, 5802: 1154–56.

Wagner, D. D., J. V. Haxby, and T. F. Heatherton. 2012. The representation of self and person knowledge in the medial prefrontal cortex. *Cognitive Science* 3, 4: 451–70.

Walton, J. 2017. The significance of consciousness studies and quantum physics for researching spirituality. *Journal for the Study of Spirituality* 7, 1: 21–34.

Ward, P. R., L. Mamerow, and S. B. Meyer. 2014. Interpersonal trust across six Asia Pacific countries: Testing and extending the "high trust society" and "low trust society". theory. *PLoS ONE* 9, 4: e95555.

Warren, J. M., N. Smith, and M. Ashwell. 2017. A structured literature review on the role of mindfulness, mindful eating, and intuitive eating in changing eating behaviours: Effectiveness and associated potential mechanisms. *Nutrition Research Reviews* 30, 2: 272–83.

Watkins, E. R. 2008. Constructive and unconstructive repetitive thought. *Psychological Bulletin* 134, 2: 163–206.

Watkins, P. C., K. Woodward, T. Stone, and R. L. Kolts. 2003. Gratitude and happiness: Development of a measure of gratitude and relationships with subjective well-being. *Social Behavior and Personality* 31, 5: 431–52.

Watson, M., A. Brennan, A. Kingstone, and J. Enns. 2010. Looking versus seeing. *Psychonomic Bulletin & Review* 17, 4: 543–49.

Watts, R. E. 2003. Reflecting as if: An integrative process in couples counseling. *Family Journal: Counseling and Therapy for Couples and Families* 11, 1: 73–75.

Watts, R. E., P. R. Peluso, and T. F. Lewis. 2005. Expanding the acting as if technique: An Adlerian/constructive integration. *Journal of Individual Psychology*, 61, 4: 380–87.

Wegner, D. M. 2002. *The Illusion of Conscious Will.* Cambridge, MA: MIT Press.

Welch, M. R., D. Sikkink, and M. T. Loveland. 2007. The radius of trust: Religion, social embeddedness, and trust in strangers. *Social Forces* 86, 1: 23–46.

Wendt, A. 1994. Collective identity formation and the international state. *American Political Science Review* 88, 2: 384–96.

Whittmann, M., S. Otten, E. Schotz, A. Sarakaya, H. Lehnen, H. G. Jo, N. Kois, S. Schmidt, and K. Meissner. 2015a. Subjective expansion of extended time spans in experienced meditators. *Frontiers in Psychology* 5: 1586.

Whittmann, M., T. Rudolph, D. Linares Gutierrez, and I. Winkler. 2015b. Time perspective and emotion regulation as predictors of age-related subjective passage of time. *International Journal of Environmental Research and Public Health* 12, 12: 16027–42.

Wichman, A. L., and A. D. Hermann. 2010. Deconstructing the link between self-doubt and self-worth: Ideas to reduce maladaptive coping. In R. M. Arkin, K. C. Oleson, and P. J. Carroll (eds.), *Handbook of the Uncertain Self*, 321–33. New York: Psychology Press.

Wilhelm, M. O., Y. Zhang, D. B. Estall, and N. H. Perdue. 2016. Raising charitable children: The effects of verbal socialization and role modeling on children's giving. *Journal of Population Economics* 30, 1: 189–24. doi:10.1007/s00148-016-0604-1.

Wilken, B., Y. Miyamoto, and Y. Uchida. 2011. Cultural influences in preference consistency: Consistency at the individual and collective levels. *Journal of Consumer Psychology* 21, 3: 346–53.

Wilson, T. W., and D. T. Gilbert. 2003. Affective forecasting. In M. P. Zanna (ed.), *Advances in Experimental Social Psychology, vol. 35*, 345–411. San Diego, CA: Academic Press.

Wisco, B. E., and S. Nolen-Hoeksema. 2011. Effect of visual perspective on memory and interpretation in dysphoria. *Behaviour Research and Therapy* 49, 6–7: 406–12.

Wisse, B., and E. Sleebos. 2016. When change causes stress: Effects of self-construal and change consequences. *Journal of Business and Psychology* 31, 2: 249–64.

Wittmann, M. 2015. Modulations of the experience of self and time. *Consciousness and Cognition* 38: 172–81.

Wood, J. V. 1989. Theory and research concerning social comparisons of personal attributes. *Psychological Bulletin* 106, 2: 231–48.

Woodruff, S., C. Glass, D. Arnkoff, K. Crowley, R. Hindman, and E. Hirschorn. 2014. Comparing self-compassion, mindfulness, and psychological inflexibility as predictors of psychological health. *Mindfulness* 5, 4: 410–21.

Woods, A. 2011. The limits of narrative: Provocations for the medical humanities. *Medical Humanities* 37, 2: 73–78.

Wulf, G. 2010. Effortless motor learning? An external focus of attention enhances movement effectiveness and efficiency. In B. Bruya (ed.), *Effortless Attention: A New Perspective in the Cognitive Science of Attention and Action*, 75–101. Cambridge, MA: MIT Press.

Xiao, Q., C. Yue, W. He, and J. Y. Yu. 2017. The mindful self: A mindfulness-enlightened self-view. *Frontiers in Psychology* 8: 1752.

Yang, J., K. Dedovic, W. Chen, and Q. Zhang. 2012. Self-esteem modulates dorsal anterior cingulate cortical response in self-referential processing. *Neuropsychologia* 50, 7: 1267–70.

Yeung, J. W. K., Z. Zhang, and T. Y. Kim. 2017. Volunteering and health benefits in general adults: Cumulative effects and forms. *BMC Public Health* 18, 1: 8.

Zauberman, G., J. Levav, K. Diehl, and R. Bhargave. 2009. 1995 feels so close yet so far: The effect of event markers on subjective feelings of time. *Psychological Science* 21, 1: 133–39.

Zauberman, G., and J. G. Lynch Jr. 2005. Resource slack and propensity to discount delayed investments of time vs. money. *Journal of Experimental Psychology: General* 134, 1: 23–37.

Zeigler-Hill, V., C. J. Holden, B. Enjaian, A. C. Southard, A. Besser, H. Li, and Q. Zhang. 2015. Self-esteem instability and personality: The connections between feelings of self-worth and the Big Five dimensions of personality. *Personality and Social Psychology Bulletin* 41, 2: 183–98.

Kate Gustin, PhD, is a clinical psychologist practicing in the San Francisco Bay Area. She received her education from Princeton University and the University of California, Berkeley, and has worked in a variety of settings over the past twenty-five years as a mental health practitioner: outpatient psychiatry, community mental health clinics, VA Hospital, college counseling services, and currently in private practice. Gustin integrates the science of positive psychology into her psychotherapy, teaching, and consultation, and leads classes and trainings for students, patients, and health care professionals.

Foreword writer **JP Sears** is an emotional healing coach, YouTuber, author, international teacher, event speaker, curious student of life, and satirist best known for his popular YouTube channel. JP's "Ultra Spiritual" videos have accumulated over 100 million online views. For more, visit www.awakenwithjp.com.

MORE BOOKS for the SPIRITUAL SEEKER

978-1572246959 / US $17.95

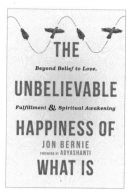

978-1626258716 / US $16.95

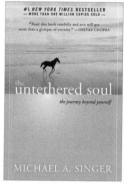

978-1572245372 / US $17.95

978-1684030156 / US $16.95